Microsoft®
Outlook® 2013
ILLUSTRATED Essentials

Microsoft®
Outlook® 2013
ILLUSTRATED Essentials

Rachel Biheller Bunin

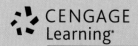
CENGAGE
Learning·

Australia · Brazil · Japan · Korea · Mexico · Singapore · Spain · United Kingdom · United States

CENGAGE
Learning®

Microsoft® Outlook® 2013—Illustrated Essentials
Rachel Biheller Bunin

Executive Editor: Marjorie Hunt

Associate Acquisitions Editor: Amanda Lyons

Senior Product Manager: Christina Kling-Garrett

Product Manager: Kim Klasner

Editorial Assistant: Brandelynn Perry

Brand Manager: Elinor Gregory

Developmental Editor: Pam Conrad

Senior Content Project Manager: Cathie DiMassa

Copyeditor: Mark Goodin

Proofreader: Lisa Weidenfeld

Indexer: Alexandra Nickerson

QA Manuscript Reviewers: John Freitas,
    Jeff Schwartz

Cover Designer: GEX Publishing Services

Cover Artist: GEX Publishing Services

Composition: GEX Publishing Services

Library of Congress Control Number: 2013936575
ISBN-13: 978-1-285-09279-9
ISBN-10: 1-285-09279-1

Cengage Learning
200 First Stamford Place, 4th Floor
Stamford, CT 06902
USA

Cengage Learning is a leading provider of customized learning solutions with office locations around the globe, including Singapore, the United Kingdom, Australia, Mexico, Brazil, and Japan. Locate your local office at: **www.cengage.com/global**

Cengage Learning products are represented in Canada by Nelson Education, Ltd.

For your course and learning solutions, visit **www.cengage.com**

Purchase any of our products at your local college store or at our preferred online store **www.cengagebrain.com**

Printed in the United States of America
1 2 3 4 5 6 7 19 18 17 16 15 14 13

Brief Contents

Preface viii

Office 2013

Unit A: Getting Started with Microsoft Office 2013 .... Office 1

Outlook 2013

Unit A: Getting Started with Email .... Outlook 1

Unit B: Managing Information Using Outlook .... Outlook 25

Cloud

Appendix: Working in the Cloud .... Cloud 1

Glossary .... Glossary 1

Index .... Index 5

Contents

Preface viii

Office 2013

Unit A: Getting Started with Microsoft Office 2013 .... **Office 1**

    Understand the Office 2013 Suite.. Office 2

        What is Office 365?

    Start an Office App.. Office 4

        Starting an app using Windows 7

        Using shortcut keys to move between Office programs

        Using the Office Clipboard

    Identify Office 2013 Screen Elements.. Office 6

        Using Backstage view

    Create and Save a File.. Office 8

        Saving files to SkyDrive

    Open a File and Save It with a New Name .... Office 10

        Exploring File Open options

        Working in Compatibility Mode

    View and Print Your Work .... Office 12

        Customizing the Quick Access toolbar

        Creating a screen capture

    Get Help, Close a File, and Exit an App... Office 14

        Enabling touch mode

        Recovering a document

    Practice .... Office 16

Outlook 2013

Unit A: Getting Started with Email... **Outlook 1**

    Communicate with Email.. Outlook 2

    Use Email Addresses .... Outlook 4

    Create and Send Emails.. Outlook 6

        Understanding message headers in emails you receive

    Understand Email Folders... Outlook 8

        Managing your email

    Receive and Reply to Emails .... Outlook 10

        Setting up vacation responses

    Forward Emails.. Outlook 12

        Controlling your message

        Flagging or labeling messages

    Send Email Attachments... Outlook 14

        Reviewing options when sending messages

    Employ Good Email Practices.. Outlook 16

        Creating distribution lists

    Practice .... Outlook 18

Unit B: Managing Information Using Outlook..**Outlook 25**

    Describe Outlook.. Outlook 26
        Weather in Calendar view

    Organize Email.. Outlook 28

    Manage Your Contacts.. Outlook 30

    Manage Your Calendar .... Outlook 32
        Sending electronic business cards

    Manage Tasks... Outlook 34

    Create Notes .... Outlook 36
        Customizing Outlook Today

    Integrate Social Connectors.. Outlook 38

    Apply Categories .... Outlook 40
        Coordinating calendars

    Practice .... Outlook 42

Cloud

Appendix: Working in the Cloud... **Cloud 1**

    Understand Office 2013 in the Cloud .... Cloud 2

    Work Online.. Cloud 4
        Getting a Microsoft account

    Explore SkyDrive .... Cloud 6
        How to disable default saving to Skydrive

    Manage Files on SkyDrive .... Cloud 8

    Share Files .... Cloud 10
        Co-authoring documents

    Explore Office Web Apps .... Cloud 12
        Exploring other Office Web Apps

    Team Project... Cloud 14

Glossary...**Glossary 1**

Index ....**Index 5**

Preface

Welcome to *Microsoft Outlook 2013—Illustrated Essentials*. This book has a unique design: Each skill is presented on two facing pages, with steps on the left and screens on the right. The layout makes it easy to learn a skill without having to read a lot of text and flip pages to see an illustration.

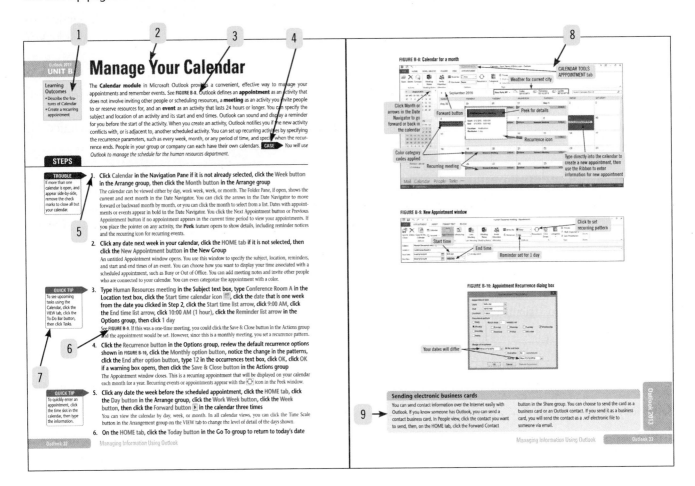

1 New! Learning Outcomes box lists measurable learning goals for which a student is accountable in that lesson.

2 Each two-page lesson focuses on a single skill.

3 Introduction briefly explains why the lesson skill is important.

4 A case scenario motivates the steps and puts learning in context.

5 Step-by-step instructions and brief explanations guide students through each hands-on lesson activity.

6 New! Figure references are now in red bold to help students refer back and forth between the steps and screenshots.

7 Tips and troubleshooting advice, right where you need it—next to the step itself.

8 New! Larger screenshots with green callouts keep students on track as they complete steps.

9 Clues to Use yellow boxes provide useful information related to the lesson skill.

This book is an ideal learning tool for a wide range of learners—the "rookies" will find the clean design easy to follow and focused with only essential information presented, and the "hotshots" will appreciate being able to move quickly through the lessons to find the information they need without reading a lot of text. The design also makes this a great reference after the course is over! See the illustration on the left to learn more about the pedagogical and design elements of a typical lesson.

What's New in this Edition

- **Coverage** — This book helps students learn the essentials of using Microsoft Outlook 2013—including using email to communicate, and using tasks, contacts, and your calendar to organize information.

- **New! Learning Outcomes** — Each lesson displays a green Learning Outcomes box that lists skills-based or knowledge-based learning goals for which students are accountable. Each Learning Outcome maps to a variety of learning activities and assessments. (See the *New! Learning Outcomes* section on page x for more information.)

- **New! Updated Design** — This edition features many new design improvements to engage students—including larger lesson screenshots with green callouts, and a refreshed Unit Opener page.

- **New! Independent Challenge 4: Explore** — This new case-based assessment activity allows students to explore new skills and use creativity to solve a problem.

Assignments

This book includes a wide variety of high quality assignments you can use for practice and assessment. Assignments include:

- **Concepts Review** — Multiple choice, matching, and screen identification questions.

- **Skills Review** — Step-by-step, hands-on review of every skill covered in the unit.

- **Independent Challenges 1–3** — Case projects requiring critical thinking and application of the unit skills. The Independent Challenges increase in difficulty. The first one in each unit provides the most hand-holding; the subsequent ones provide less guidance and require more critical thinking and independent problem solving.

- **Independent Challenge 4: Explore** — Case projects that let students explore new skills that are related to the core skills covered in the unit and are often more open ended, allowing students to use creativity to complete the assignment.

- **Visual Workshop** — Critical thinking exercises that require students to create a project by looking at a completed solution; they must apply the skills they've learned in the unit and use critical thinking skills to create the project from scratch.

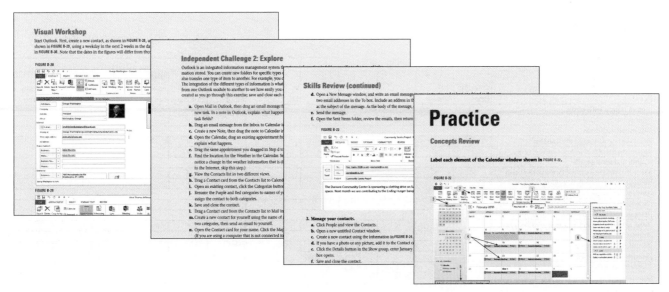

New! Learning Outcomes

Every 2-page lesson in this book now contains a green **Learning Outcomes box** that states the learning goals for that lesson.

- **What is a learning outcome?** A learning outcome states what a student is expected to know or be able to do after completing a lesson. Each learning outcome is skills-based or knowledge-based and is *measurable*. Learning outcomes map to learning activities and assessments.

- **How do students benefit from learning outcomes?** Learning outcomes tell students exactly what skills and knowledge they are *accountable* for learning in that lesson. This helps students study more efficiently and effectively and makes them more active learners.

- **How do instructors benefit from learning outcomes?** Learning outcomes provide clear, measurable, skills-based learning goals that map to various high-quality learning activities and assessments. A **Learning Outcomes Map**, available for each unit in this book, maps every learning outcome to the learning activities and assessments shown below.

Learning Outcomes Map to These Learning Activities:

- **Book lessons:** Step-by-step tutorial on one skill presented in a two-page learning format.

Learning Outcomes Map to These Assessments:

1. **End-of-Unit Exercises: Concepts Review** (screen identification, matching, multiple choice); **Skills Review** (hands-on review of each lesson); **Independent Challenges** (hands-on, case-based review of specific skills); **Visual Workshop** (activity that requires student to build a project by looking at a picture of the final solution).

2. **Exam View Test Banks:** Objective-based questions you can use for online or paper testing.

Learning Outcomes Map

A **Learning Outcomes Map**, contained in the Instructor Resources, provides a listing of learning activities and assessments for each learning outcome in the book.

Learning Outcomes Map
Microsoft Outlook 2013
Unit A

EIC=Extra Independent Challenge

	Concepts Review	Skills Review	IC1	IC2	VW	EIC 1	EIC 2	Test Bank	SAM Assessment	SAM Projects	SAM Training	Illustrated Video
Communicate with email												
Identify the benefits of email		✓	✓	✓	✓			✓				
Use email addresses												
Know the four parts of an email address	✓	✓	✓	✓				✓				
Explain the benefits of an email address book		✓	✓	✓	✓			✓				
Create and send emails												
Enter email addresses in the To and Cc text boxes	✓	✓	✓	✓	✓			✓				
Write and send an email message		✓	✓	✓	✓			✓				
Understand email folders												
Describe the purpose of each Outlook default folder	✓	✓						✓				
Receive and reply to emails												
Send, receive, view, and reply to an email message		✓	✓	✓	✓			✓				
Forward emails												
Forward an email message		✓	✓	✓				✓				
Send email attachments												
Use Autocomplete to add an ...		✓	✓	✓								
Attach a fil...												

Instructor Resources

This book comes with a wide array of high-quality technology-based, teaching tools to help you teach and to help students learn. The following teaching tools are available for download at our Instructor Companion Site. Simply search for this text at *login.cengage.com*. An instructor login is required.

- **New! Learning Outcomes Map** — A detailed grid for each unit (in Excel format) shows the learning activities and assessments that map to each learning outcome in that unit.

- **Instructor's Manual** — Available as an electronic file, the Instructor's Manual includes lecture notes with teaching tips for each unit.

- **Sample Syllabus** — Prepare and customize your course easily using this sample course outline.

- **PowerPoint Presentations** — Each unit has a corresponding PowerPoint presentation covering the skills and topics in that unit that you can use in lectures, distribute to your students, or customize to suit your course.

- **Figure Files** — The figures in the text are provided on the Instructor Resources site to help you illustrate key topics or concepts. You can use these to create your own slide shows or learning tools.

- **Solution Files** — Solution Files are files that contain the finished project that students create or modify in the lessons or end-of-unit material.

- **Solutions Document** — This document outlines the solutions for the end-of-unit Concepts Review, Skills Review, Independent Challenges and Visual Workshops. An Annotated Solution File and Grading Rubric accompany each file and can be used together for efficient grading.

- **ExamView Test Banks** — ExamView is a powerful testing software package that allows you to create and administer printed, computer (LAN-based), and Internet exams. Our ExamView test banks include questions that correspond to the skills and concepts covered in this text, enabling students to generate detailed study guides that include page references for further review. The computer-based and Internet testing components allow students to take exams at their computers, and also save you time by grading each exam automatically.

Key Facts About Using This Book

Data Files are needed: To complete many of the lessons and end-of-unit assignments, students need to start from partially completed Data Files, which help students learn more efficiently. By starting out with a Data File, students can focus on performing specific tasks without having to create a file from scratch. All Data Files are available as part of the Instructor Resources. Students can also download Data Files themselves for free at cengagebrain.com. (For detailed instructions, go to www.cengage.com/ct/studentdownload.)

System requirements: This book was developed using Microsoft Office 2013 Professional running on Windows 8. Note that Windows 8 is not a requirement for the units on Microsoft Office; Office 2013 runs virtually the same on Windows 7 and Windows 8. Please see Important Notes for Windows 7 Users on page xv for more information.

Screen resolution: This book was written and tested on computers with monitors set at a resolution of 1366 x 768. If your screen shows more or less information than the figures in this book, your monitor is probably set at a higher or lower resolution. If you don't see something on your screen, you might have to scroll down or up to see the object identified in the figure.

Tell Us What You Think!

We want to hear from you! Please email your questions, comments, and suggestions to the Illustrated Series team at: **illustratedseries@cengage.com**

CENGAGE**brain**.com

Buy. Rent. Access.

Access Student Data Files and other
study tools on **cengagebrain.com**.

For detailed instructions visit
www.cengage.com/ct/studentdownload.

Store your Data Files on a USB drive for maximum efficiency in
organizing and working with the files.

Macintosh users should use a program to expand WinZip or PKZip archives.
Ask your instructor or lab coordinator for assistance.

Other Illustrated Titles

 Microsoft® Office 2013 -
Illustrated Fundamentals
**Marjorie Hunt/Barbara Clemens
(9781285418292)**

 Microsoft® Access® 2013 -
Illustrated Complete
Lisa Friedrichsen (9781285093277)

 Microsoft® Office 2013 -
Illustrated Introductory,
First Course
**Beskeen/Cram/Duffy/
Friedrichsen/Reding
(9781285088457)**

 Microsoft® Excel® 2013 -
Illustrated Complete
**Elizabeth Eisner Reding/Lynn
Wermers (9781285093192)**

 Microsoft® Office 2013 -
Illustrated Second Course
**Beskeen/Cram/Duffy/
Friedrichsen/Wermers
(9781285082257)**

 Microsoft® PowerPoint® 2013 -
Illustrated Introductory
**David W. Beskeen
(9781285082592)**

 Microsoft® Office 2013 -
Illustrated Third Course
**Cram/Friedrichsen/Wermers
(9781285082462)**

 Microsoft® Word 2013 -
Illustrated Complete
**Jennifer Duffy/Carol Cram
(9781285093116)**

Acknowledgements

Author Acknowledgements

Thank you to Marjorie Hunt, Christina Kling-Garrett, and Cathie DiMassa at Cengage Learning for their hard work and for making this book possible. Appreciation to my awesome colleague and development editor, Pam Conrad, for her keen eye and wonderful suggestions. My special thanks to David, Jennifer, Emily, and Michael.

Rachel Biheller Bunin

Advisory Board Acknowledgements

We thank our Illustrated Advisory Board who gave us their opinions and guided our decisions as we developed all of the new editions for Microsoft Office 2013.

Merlin Amirtharaj, Stanly Community College

Londo Andrews, J. Sargeant Reynolds Community College

Rachelle Hall, Glendale Community College

Terri Helfand, Chaffey Community College

Sheryl Lenhart, Terra Community College

Dr. Jose Nieves, Lord Fairfax Community College

Coming Soon: MindTap

MindTap is a fully online, highly personalized learning experience built upon Cengage Learning content. MindTap combines student learning tools—readings, multimedia, activities and assessments—into a singular Learning Path that guides students through their course. Instructors personalize the experience by customizing authoritative Cengage Learning content and learning tools, including the ability to add SAM trainings, assessments, and projects into the Learning Path via a SAM app that integrates into the MindTap framework seamlessly with Learning Management Systems. Available in 2014.

Important Notes for Windows 7 Users

The screenshots in this book show Microsoft Office 2013 running on Windows 8. However, if you are using Microsoft Windows 7, you can still use this book because Office 2013 runs virtually the same on both platforms. There are only two differences that you will encounter if you are using Windows 7. Read this section to understand the differences.

Dialog boxes

If you are a Windows 7 user, dialog boxes shown in this book will look slightly different than what you see on your screen. Dialog boxes for Windows 7 have a light blue title bar, instead of a medium blue title bar. However, beyond this superficial difference in appearance, the options in the dialog boxes across platforms are the same. For instance, the screen shots below show the Font dialog box running on Windows 7 and the Font dialog box running on Windows 8.

FIGURE 1: **Font dialog box in Windows 7**

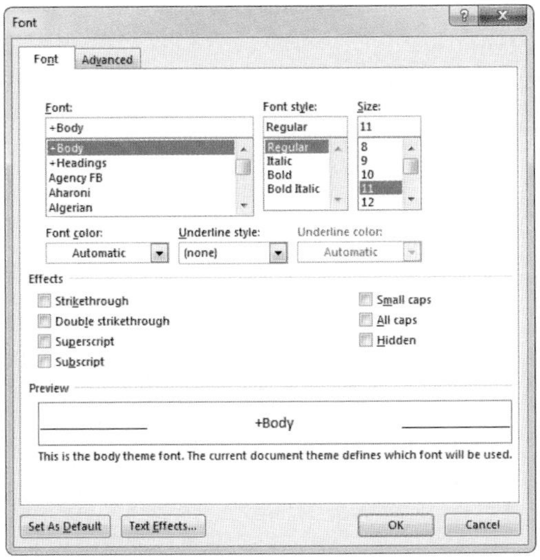

FIGURE 2: **Font dialog box in Windows 8**

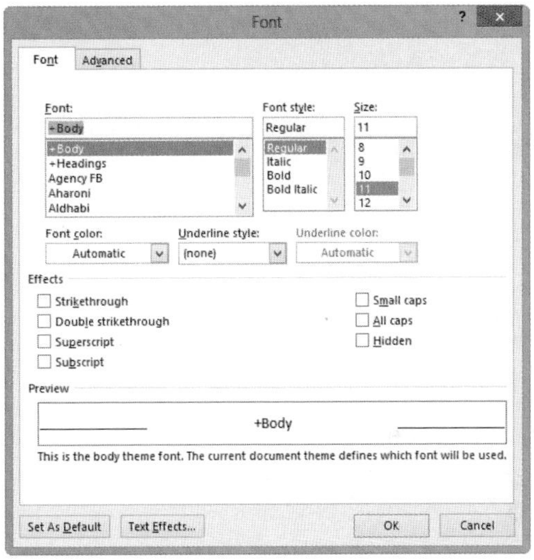

Alternate Steps for Starting an App in Windows 7

Nearly all of the steps in this book work exactly the same for Windows 7 users. However, starting an app (or program/application) requires different steps for Windows 7. The steps below show the Windows 7 steps for starting an app. (Note: Windows 7 alternate steps also appear in red Trouble boxes next to any step in the book that requires starting an app.)

Starting an app (or program/application) using Windows 7

1. Click the **Start button** on the taskbar to open the Start menu.
2. Click **All Programs**, then click the **Microsoft Office 2013 folder**. See Figure 3.
3. Click the app you want to use (such as **Excel 2013**).

FIGURE 3: **Starting an app using Windows 7**

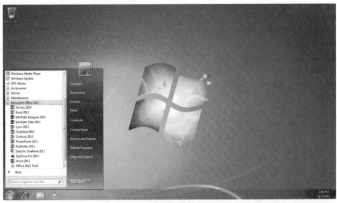

Getting Started with Microsoft Office 2013

CASE This unit introduces you to the most frequently used programs in Office, as well as common features they all share.

Unit Objectives

After completing this unit, you will be able to:

- Understand the Office 2013 suite
- Start an Office app
- Identify Office 2013 screen elements
- Create and save a file

- Open a file and save it with a new name
- View and print your work
- Get Help, close a file, and exit an app

File You Will Need

OFFICE A-1.xlsx

Understand the Office 2013 Suite

Learning Outcomes
• Identify Office suite components
• Describe the features of each program

Microsoft Office 2013 is a group of programs--which are also called applications or apps--designed to help you create documents, collaborate with coworkers, and track and analyze information. You use different Office programs to accomplish specific tasks, such as writing a letter or producing a presentation, yet all the programs have a similar look and feel. Microsoft Office 2013 apps feature a common, context-sensitive user interface, so you can get up to speed faster and use advanced features with greater ease. The Office apps are bundled together in a group called a **suite**. The Office suite is available in several configurations, but all include Word, Excel, and PowerPoint. Other configurations include Access, Outlook, Publisher, and other programs. **CASE** ▸ As part of your job, you need to understand how each Office app is best used to complete specific tasks.

DETAILS

The Office apps covered in this book include:

• **Microsoft Word 2013**

When you need to create any kind of text-based document, such as a memo, newsletter, or multipage report, Word is the program to use. You can easily make your documents look great by inserting eye-catching graphics and using formatting tools such as themes, which are available in most Office programs. **Themes** are predesigned combinations of color and formatting attributes you can apply to a document. The Word document shown in **FIGURE A-1** was formatted with the Organic theme.

• **Microsoft Excel 2013**

Excel is the perfect solution when you need to work with numeric values and make calculations. It puts the power of formulas, functions, charts, and other analytical tools into the hands of every user, so you can analyze sales projections, calculate loan payments, and present your findings in a professional manner. The Excel worksheet shown in **FIGURE A-1** tracks personal expenses. Because Excel automatically recalculates results whenever a value changes, the information is always up to date. A chart illustrates how the monthly expenses are broken down.

• **Microsoft PowerPoint 2013**

Using PowerPoint, it's easy to create powerful presentations complete with graphics, transitions, and even a soundtrack. Using professionally designed themes and clip art, you can quickly and easily create dynamic slide shows such as the one shown in **FIGURE A-1**.

• **Microsoft Access 2013**

Access is a relational database program that helps you keep track of large amounts of quantitative data, such as product inventories or employee records. The form shown in **FIGURE A-1** was created for a grocery store inventory database. Employees use the form to enter data about each item. Using Access enables employees to quickly find specific information such as price and quantity.

Microsoft Office has benefits beyond the power of each program, including:

• **Common user interface: Improving business processes**

Because the Office suite programs have a similar **interface**, or look and feel, your experience using one program's tools makes it easy to learn those in the other programs. In addition, Office documents are **compatible** with one another, meaning that you can easily incorporate, or **integrate**, an Excel chart into a PowerPoint slide, or an Access table into a Word document.

• **Collaboration: Simplifying how people work together**

Office recognizes the way people do business today, and supports the emphasis on communication and knowledge sharing within companies and across the globe. All Office programs include the capability to incorporate feedback—called **online collaboration**—across the Internet or a company network.

FIGURE A-1: Microsoft Office 2013 documents

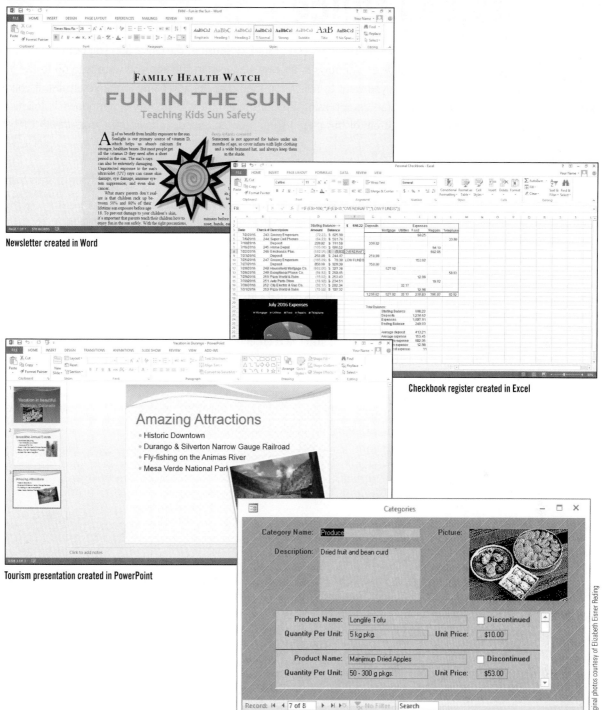

Newsletter created in Word

Checkbook register created in Excel

Tourism presentation created in PowerPoint

Store inventory form created in Access

What is Office 365?

Until the release of Microsoft Office 2013, most consumers purchased Microsoft Office in a traditional way: by buying a retail package from a store or downloading it from Microsoft. com. You can still purchase Microsoft Office 2013 in this traditional way--but you can also now purchase it as a subscription service called Microsoft Office 365 (for businesses) and Microsoft Office 365 Home Premium (for consumers). Office 365 requires businesses to pay a subscription fee for each user. Office 365 Home Premium Edition allows households to install Office on up to 5 devices. These subscription versions of Office provide extra services and are optimized for working in the cloud.

Start an Office App

Learning Outcomes
• Start an Office app
• Explain the purpose of a template
• Start a new blank document

To get started using Microsoft Office, you need to start, or **launch**, the Office app you want to use. If you are running Microsoft Office on Windows 8, an easy way to start the app you want is to go to the Start screen, type the app name you want to search for, then click the app name In the Results list. If you are running Windows 7, you start an app using the Start menu. (If you are running Windows 7, follow the Windows 7 steps at the bottom of this page.) **CASE** ▶ *You decide to familiarize yourself with Office by starting Microsoft Word.*

STEPS

TROUBLE
If you are running Windows 7, follow the steps in the yellow box below.

1. **Go to the** Windows 8 Start screen

   Your screen displays a variety of colorful tiles for all the apps on your computer. You could locate the app you want to open by scrolling to the right until you see it, or you can type the app name to search for it.

2. **Type** word

   Your screen now displays "Word 2013" under "Results for 'word'", along with any other app that has "word" as part of its name (such as WordPad). See **FIGURE A-2**.

3. **Click** Word 2013

   Word 2013 launches, and the Word **start screen** appears, as shown in **FIGURE A-3**. The start screen is a landing page that appears when you first start an Office app. The left side of this screen displays recent files you have opened. (If you have never opened any files, then there will be no files listed under Recent.) The right side displays images depicting different templates you can use to create different types of documents. A **template** is a file containing professionally designed content that you can easily replace with your own. You can also start from scratch using the Blank Document option.

Starting an app using Windows 7

1. **Click the** Start button ⊕ **on the taskbar**
2. **Click** All Programs **on the Start menu, click the** Microsoft Office 2013 folder **as shown in FIGURE A-4, then click** Word 2013

Word 2013 launches, and the Word start screen appears, as shown previously in **FIGURE A-3**. The start screen is a landing page that appears when you first start an Office app. The left side of this screen displays recent files you have opened. (If you have never opened any files, then there will be no files listed under Recent.) The right side displays images depicting different templates you can use to create different types of documents. A **template** is a file containing professionally designed content that you can easily replace with your own. Using a template to create a document can save time and ensure that your document looks great. You can also start from scratch using the Blank Document option.

Using shortcut keys to move between Office programs

You can switch between open apps using a keyboard shortcut. The [Alt][Tab] keyboard combination lets you either switch quickly to the next open program or file or choose one from a gallery. To switch immediately to the next open program or file, press [Alt][Tab]. To choose from all open programs and files, press and hold [Alt], then press and release [Tab] without releasing [Alt]. A gallery opens on screen, displaying the filename and a thumbnail image of each open program and file, as well as of the desktop. Each time you press [Tab] while holding [Alt], the selection cycles to the next open file or location. Release [Alt] when the program, file, or location you want to activate is selected.

FIGURE A-2: Searching for Word app from the Start screen in Windows 8

Word 2013 app appears as a search result when you type "word"

FIGURE A-3: Word start screen

Your name will appear here if you signed in using a Microsoft account

Recently opened documents appear here

Templates let you create a certain type of document fast using professionally designed content you can modify

FIGURE A-4: Starting an app using Windows 7

Using the Office Clipboard

You can use the Office Clipboard to cut and copy items from one Office program and paste them into others. The Office Clipboard can store a maximum of 24 items. To access it, open the Office Clipboard task pane by clicking the dialog box launcher 🔲 in the Clipboard group on the HOME tab. Each time you copy a selection, it is saved in the Office Clipboard. Each entry in the Office Clipboard includes an icon that tells you the program it was created in. To paste an entry, click in the document where you want it to appear, then click the item in the Office Clipboard. To delete an item from the Office Clipboard, right-click the item, then click Delete.

Identify Office 2013 Screen Elements

Learning Outcomes
- Identify basic components of the user interface
- Display and use Backstage view
- Adjust the Zoom level

One of the benefits of using Office is that the programs have much in common, making them easy to learn and making it simple to move from one to another. Individual Office programs have always shared many features, but the innovations in the Office 2013 user interface mean even greater similarity among them all. That means you can also use your knowledge of one program to get up to speed in another. A **user interface** is a collective term for all the ways you interact with a software program. The user interface in Office 2013 provides intuitive ways to choose commands, work with files, and navigate in the program window. **CASE** *Familiarize yourself with some of the common interface elements in Office by examining the PowerPoint program window.*

STEPS

1. **Go to the Windows 8 Start screen, type pow, click PowerPoint 2013, then click Blank Presentation**

   PowerPoint becomes the active program displaying a blank slide. Refer to **FIGURE A-5** to identify common elements of the Office user interface. The **document window** occupies most of the screen. At the top of every Office program window is a **title bar** that displays the document name and program name. Below the title bar is the **Ribbon**, which displays commands you're likely to need for the current task. Commands are organized onto **tabs**. The tab names appear at the top of the Ribbon, and the active tab appears in front.

2. **Click the FILE tab**

   The FILE tab opens, displaying **Backstage view**. It is called Backstage view becausee the commands available here are for working with the files "behind the scenes." The navigation bar on the left side of Backstage view contains commands to perform actions common to most Office programs.

3. **Click the Back button ⊙ to close Backstage view and return to the document window, then click the DESIGN tab on the Ribbon**

   To display a different tab, click its name. Each tab contains related commands arranged into **groups** to make features easy to find. On the DESIGN tab, the Themes group displays available design themes in a **gallery**, or visual collection of choices you can browse. Many groups contain a **dialog box launcher**, which you can click to open a dialog box or pane from which to choose related commands.

4. **Move the mouse pointer ⩗ over the Ion theme in the Themes group as shown in FIGURE A-6, but *do not click* the mouse button**

   The Ion theme is temporarily applied to the slide in the document window. However, because you did not click the theme, you did not permanently change the slide. With the **Live Preview** feature, you can point to a choice, see the results, then decide if you want to make the change. Live Preview is available throughout Office.

5. **Move ⩗ away from the Ribbon and towards the slide**

   If you had clicked the Ion theme, it would be applied to this slide. Instead, the slide remains unchanged.

6. **Point to the Zoom slider ▬▬▬▬▬▬ 100% on the status bar, then drag to the right until the Zoom level reads 166%**

   The slide display is enlarged. Zoom tools are located on the status bar. You can drag the slider or click the Zoom In or Zoom Out buttons to zoom in or out on an area of interest. **Zooming in** (a higher percentage), makes a document appear bigger on screen but less of it fits on the screen at once; **zooming out** (a lower percentage) lets you see more of the document at a reduced size.

7. **Click the Zoom Out button ▬ on the status bar to the left of the Zoom slider until the Zoom level reads 120%**

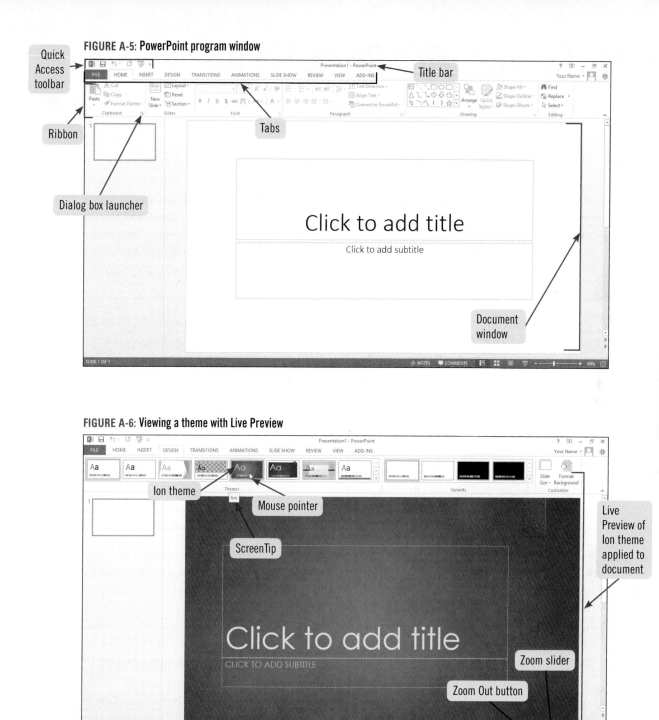

FIGURE A-5: PowerPoint program window

Quick Access toolbar

Ribbon

Dialog box launcher

Tabs

Title bar

Click to add title

Click to add subtitle

Document window

FIGURE A-6: Viewing a theme with Live Preview

Ion theme

Mouse pointer

ScreenTip

Live Preview of Ion theme applied to document

Click to add title

CLICK TO ADD SUBTITLE

Zoom slider

Zoom Out button

Zoom In button

Zoom percentage

Using Backstage view

Backstage view in each Microsoft Office program offers "one stop shopping" for many commonly performed tasks, such as opening and saving a file, printing and previewing a document, defining document properties, sharing information, and exiting a program. Backstage view opens when you click the FILE tab in any Office program, and while features such as the Ribbon, Mini toolbar, and Live Preview all help you work *in* your documents, the FILE tab and Backstage view help you work *with* your documents. You can return to your active document by pressing the Back button.

Create and Save a File

Learning
Outcomes
• Create a file
• Save a file
• Explain SkyDrive

When working in an Office program, one of the first things you need to do is to create and save a file. A **file** is a stored collection of data. Saving a file enables you to work on a project now, then put it away and work on it again later. In some Office programs, including Word, Excel, and PowerPoint, you can open a new file when you start the program, then all you have to do is enter some data and save it. In Access, you must create a file before you enter any data. You should give your files meaningful names and save them in an appropriate location, such as a folder on your hard drive or SkyDrive so they're easy to find. **SkyDrive** is the Microsoft cloud storage system that lets you easily save, share, and access your files from anywhere you have Internet access. See "Saving Files to SkyDrive" for more information on this topic. **CASE** ▶ *Use Word to familiarize yourself with creating and saving a document. First you'll type some notes about a possible location for a corporate meeting, then you'll save the information for later use.*

STEPS

1. **Click the Word program button [w] on the taskbar, click Blank document, then click the Zoom In button [+] until the level is 120%, if necessary**

2. **Type Locations for Corporate Meeting, then press [Enter] twice**
   The text appears in the document window, and the **insertion point** blinks on a new blank line. The insertion point indicates where the next typed text will appear.

3. **Type Las Vegas, NV, press [Enter], type San Diego, CA, press [Enter], type Seattle, WA, press [Enter] twice, then type your name**

4. **Click the Save button [💾] on the Quick Access toolbar**
   Backstage view opens showing various options for saving the file, as shown in **FIGURE A-7**.

5. **Click Computer, then click Browse**
   Because this is the first time you are saving this document, the Save As command is displayed. Once you choose a location where you will save the file, the Save As dialog box displays, as shown in **FIGURE A-8**. Once a file is saved, clicking [💾] saves any changes to the file *without* opening the Save As dialog box. The Address bar in the Save As dialog box displays the default location for saving the file, but you can change it to any location. The File name field contains a suggested name for the document based on text in the file, but you can enter a different name.

6. **Type OF A-Potential Corporate Meeting Locations**
   The text you type replaces the highlighted text. (The "OF A-" in the filename indicates that the file is created in Office Unit A. You will see similar designations throughout this book when files are named.)

7. **In the Save As dialog box, use the Address bar or Navigation Pane to navigate to the location where you store your Data Files**
   You can store files on your computer, a network drive, your SkyDrive, or any acceptable storage device.

8. **Click Save**
   The Save As dialog box closes, the new file is saved to the location you specified, and the name of the document appears in the title bar, as shown in **FIGURE A-9**. (You may or may not see the file extension ".docx" after the filename.) See **TABLE A-1** for a description of the different types of files you create in Office, and the file extensions associated with each.

TABLE A-1: Common filenames and default file extensions

file created in	is called a	and has the default extension
Word	document	.docx
Excel	workbook	.xlsx
PowerPoint	presentation	.pptx
Access	database	.accdb

FIGURE A-7: Save As screen in Backstage view

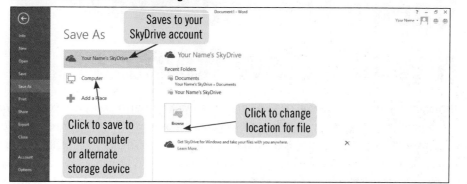

Saves to your SkyDrive account

Click to save to your computer or alternate storage device

Click to change location for file

FIGURE A-8: Save As dialog box

Address bar

Navigation pane; your links and folders may differ

File name field; your computer may not display file extensions

Save as type list

FIGURE A-9: Saved and named Word document

Save button

File name appears in title bar

Locations for Corporate Meeting

Las Vegas, NV

San Diego, CA

Seattle, WA

Your name should appear here

Your Name

Insertion point

Saving files to SkyDrive

All Office programs include the capability to incorporate feedback—called **online collaboration**—across the Internet or a company network. Using **cloud computing** (work done in a virtual environment), you can take advantage of commonly shared features such as a consistent interface. Using SkyDrive, a free file storage service from Microsoft, you and your colleagues can create and store documents in the cloud and make the documents available anywhere there is Internet access to whomever you choose. To use SkyDrive, you need a free Microsoft Account, which you obtain at the signup.live.com website. You can find more information about SkyDrive in the "Working in the Cloud" appendix. When you are logged into your Microsoft account and you save a file in any of

the Office apps, the first option in the Save As screen is your SkyDrive. Double-click your SkyDrive option and the Save As dialog box opens displaying a location in the address bar unique to your SkyDrive account. Type a name in the File name text box, then click Save and your file is saved to your SkyDrive. To sync your files with SkyDrive, you'll need to download and install the SkyDrive for Windows app. Then, when you open Explorer, you'll notice a new folder called SkyDrive has been added to the Users folder. In this folder is a sub-folder called Documents, in which an updated copy of your Office app files resides. This means if your Internet connection fails, you can work on your files offline. The SkyDrive folder also displays Explorer in the list of Favorites folders.

Open a File and Save It with a New Name

Learning Outcomes
• Open an existing file
• Save a file with a new name

In many cases as you work in Office, you start with a blank document, but often you need to use an existing file. It might be a file you or a coworker created earlier as a work in progress, or it could be a complete document that you want to use as the basis for another. For example, you might want to create a budget for this year using the budget you created last year; instead of typing in all the categories and information from scratch, you could open last year's budget, save it with a new name, and just make changes to update it for the current year. By opening the existing file and saving it with the Save As command, you create a duplicate that you can modify to suit your needs, while the original file remains intact. **CASE** ▶ *Use Excel to open an existing workbook file, and save it with a new name so the original remains unchanged.*

STEPS

> **TROUBLE**
> If you are running WIndows 7, click the Start button on the taskbar, type excel, then click Excel 2013.

1. **Go to the Windows 8 Start screen, type exc, click Excel 2013, click Open Other Workbooks, click Computer on the navigation bar, then click Browse**

   The Open dialog box opens, where you can navigate to any drive or folder accessible to your computer to locate a file. You can click Recent Workbooks on the navigation bar to display a list of recent workbooks; click a file in the list to open it.

2. **In the Open dialog box, navigate to the location where you store your Data Files**

   The files available in the current folder are listed, as shown in **FIGURE A-10**. This folder displays one file.

> **TROUBLE**
> Click Enable Editing on the Protected View bar near the top of your document window if prompted.

3. **Click OFFICE A-1.xlsx, then click Open**

   The dialog box closes, and the file opens in Excel. An Excel file is an electronic spreadsheet, so the new file displays a grid of rows and columns you can use to enter and organize data.

4. **Click the FILE tab, click Save As on the navigation bar, then click Browse**

   The Save As dialog box opens, and the current filename is highlighted in the File name text box. Using the Save As command enables you to create a copy of the current, existing file with a new name. This action preserves the original file and creates a new file that you can modify.

5. **Navigate to the location where you store your Data Files if necessary, type OF A-Budget for Corporate Meeting in the File name text box, as shown in FIGURE A-11, then click Save**

   A copy of the existing workbook is created with the new name. The original file, Office A-1.xlsx, closes automatically.

6. **Click cell A19, type your name, then press [Enter], as shown in FIGURE A-12**

   In Excel, you enter data in cells, which are formed by the intersection of a row and a column. Cell A19 is at the intersection of column A and row 19. When you press [Enter], the cell pointer moves to cell A20.

7. **Click the Save button 🖫 on the Quick Access toolbar**

   Your name appears in the workbook, and your changes to the file are saved.

Exploring File Open options

You might have noticed that the Open button in the Open dialog box includes a list arrow to the right of the button. In a dialog box, if a button includes a list arrow you can click the button to invoke the command, or you can click the list arrow to see a list of related commands that you can apply to a selected file in the file list. The Open list arrow includes several related commands, including Open Read-Only and Open as Copy.

Clicking Open Read-Only opens a file that you can only save with a new name; you cannot make changes to the original file. Clicking Open as Copy creates and opens a copy of the selected file and inserts the word "Copy" in the file's title. Like the Save As command, these commands provide additional ways to use copies of existing files while ensuring that original files do not get changed by mistake.

FIGURE A-10: Open dialog box

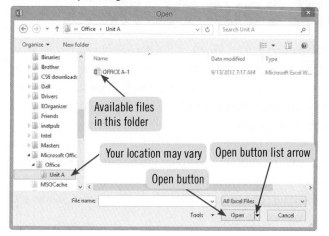

FIGURE A-11: Save As dialog box

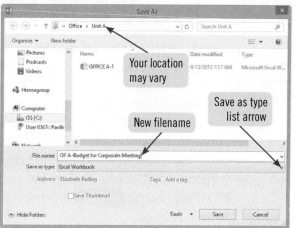

FIGURE A-12: Your name added to the workbook

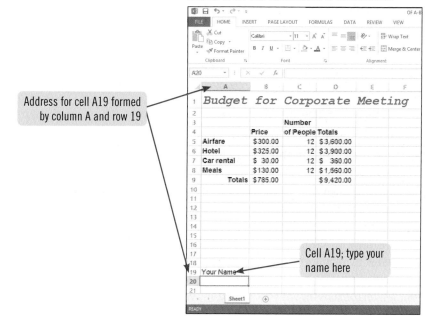

Working in Compatibility Mode

Not everyone upgrades to the newest version of Office. As a general rule, new software versions are **backward compatible**, meaning that documents saved by an older version can be read by newer software. To open documents created in older Office versions, Office 2013 includes a feature called Compatibility Mode. When you use Office 2013 to open a file created in an earlier version of Office, "Compatibility Mode" appears in the title bar, letting you know the file was created in an earlier but usable version of the program. If you are working with someone who may not be using the newest version of the software, you can avoid possible incompatibility problems by saving your file in another, earlier format. To do this in an Office program, click the FILE tab, click Save As on the navigation bar, click the location where you want to save the file, then click Browse. In the Save As dialog box, click the Save as type list arrow in the Save As dialog box, then click an option on the list. For example, if you're working in Excel, click Excel 97-2003 Workbook format in the Save as type list to save an Excel file so it can be opened in Excel 97 or Excel 2003.

View and Print Your Work

Learning
Outcomes
• Describe and
change views in
an app
• Print a document

Each Microsoft Office program lets you switch among various **views** of the document window to show more or fewer details or a different combination of elements that make it easier to complete certain tasks, such as formatting or reading text. Changing your view of a document does not affect the file in any way, it affects only the way it looks on screen. If your computer is connected to a printer or a print server, you can easily print any Office document using the Print button on the Print tab in Backstage view. Printing can be as simple as **previewing** the document to see exactly what a document will look like when it is printed and then clicking the Print button. Or, you can customize the print job by printing only selected pages. The Backstage view can also be used to share your document with others, or to export it in a different format. **CASE** *Experiment with changing your view of a Word document, and then preview and print your work.*

STEPS

1. **Click the Word program button ■ on the taskbar**

   Word becomes the active program, and the document fills the screen.

2. **Click the VIEW tab on the Ribbon**

   In most Office programs, the VIEW tab on the Ribbon includes groups and commands for changing your view of the current document. You can also change views using the View buttons on the status bar.

3. **Click the Read Mode button in the Views group on the VIEW tab**

   The view changes to Read Mode view, as shown in **FIGURE A-13**. This view shows the document in an easy-to-read, distraction-free reading mode. Notice that the Ribbon is no longer visible on screen.

4. **Click the Print Layout button ▤ on the Status bar**

   You return to Print Layout view, the default view in Word.

5. **Click the FILE tab, then click Print on the navigation bar**

   The Print tab opens in Backstage view. The preview pane on the right side of the window displays a preview of how your document will look when printed. Compare your screen to **FIGURE A-14**. Options in the Settings section enable you to change margins, orientation, and paper size before printing. To change a setting, click it, and then click a new setting. For instance, to change from Letter paper size to Legal, click Letter in the Settings section, then click Legal on the menu that opens. The document preview updates as you change the settings. You also can use the Settings section to change which pages to print. If your computer is connected to multiple printers, you can click the current printer in the Printer section, then click the one you want to use. The Print section contains the Print button and also enables you to select the number of copies of the document to print.

6. **If your school allows printing, click the Print button in the Print section (otherwise, click the Back button ⊙)**

   If you chose to print, a copy of the document prints, and Backstage view closes.

Customizing the Quick Access toolbar

You can customize the Quick Access toolbar to display your favorite commands. To do so, click the Customize Quick Access Toolbar button ▾ in the title bar, then click the command you want to add. If you don't see the command in the list, click More Commands to open the Quick Access Toolbar tab of the current program's Options dialog box. In the Options dialog box, use the Choose commands from list to choose a category, click the desired command in the list on the left, click Add to add it to the Quick Access toolbar, then click OK. To remove a button from the toolbar, click the name in the list on the right in the Options dialog box, then click Remove. To add a command to the Quick Access toolbar as you work, simply right-click the button on the Ribbon, then click Add to Quick Access Toolbar on the shortcut menu. To move the Quick Access toolbar below the Ribbon, click the Customize Quick Access Toolbar button, and then click Show Below the Ribbon.

FIGURE A-13: Web Layout view

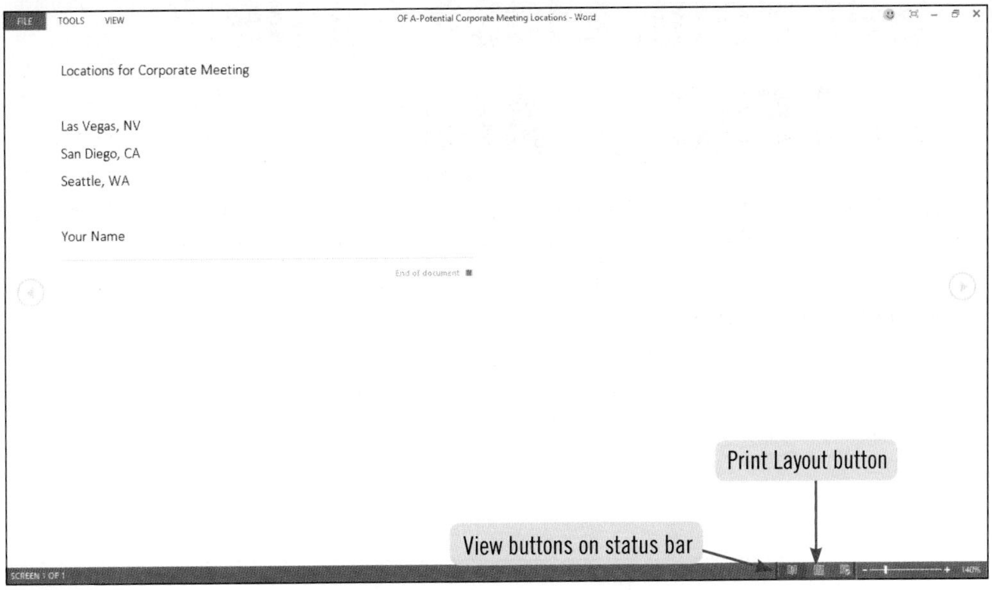

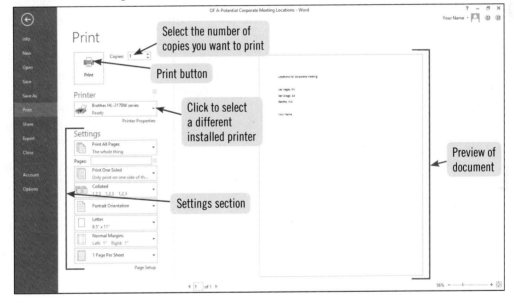

Print Layout button

View buttons on status bar

FIGURE A-14: Print settings on the FILE tab

Select the number of copies you want to print

Print button

Click to select a different installed printer

Settings section

Preview of document

Creating a screen capture

A **screen capture** is a digital image of your screen, as if you took a picture of it with a camera. For instance, you might want to take a screen capture if an error message occurs and you want a Technical Support person to see exactly what's on the screen. You can create a screen capture using features found in Windows 8 or Office 2013. Both Windows 7 and Windows 8 come with the Snipping Tool, a separate program designed to capture whole screens or portions of screens. To open the Snipping Tool, click the Start screen thumbnail, type "sni", then click the Snipping Tool when it appears in the left panel. After opening the Snipping Tool, click New, then drag the pointer on the screen to select the area of the screen you want to capture. When you release the mouse button, the screen capture opens in the Snipping Tool window, and you can save, copy, or send it in an email. In Word, Excel, and PowerPoint 2013, you can capture screens or portions of screens and insert them in the current document using the Screenshot button in the Illustrations group on the INSERT tab. And finally, you can create a screen capture by pressing [PrtScn]. (Keyboards differ, but you may find the [PrtScn] button in or near your keyboard's function keys.) Pressing this key places a digital image of your screen in the Windows temporary storage area known as the **Clipboard**. Open the document where you want the screen capture to appear, click the HOME tab on the Ribbon (if necessary), then click the Paste button in the Clipboard group on the HOME tab. The screen capture is pasted into the document.

Office 2013

Get Help, Close a File, and Exit an App

Learning
Outcomes
•Display a
 ScreenTip
•Use Help
•Close a file
•Exit an app

You can get comprehensive help at any time by pressing [F1] in an Office app or clicking the Help button on the right end of the title bar. You can also get help in the form of a ScreenTip by pointing to almost any icon in the program window. When you're finished working in an Office document, you have a few choices regarding ending your work session. You close a file by clicking the FILE tab, then clicking Close; you exit a program by clicking the Close button on the title bar. Closing a file leaves a program running, while exiting a program closes all the open files in that program as well as the program itself. In all cases, Office reminds you if you try to close a file or exit a program and your document contains unsaved changes. **CASE** ▶ *Explore the Help system in Microsoft Office, and then close your documents and exit any open programs.*

STEPS

1. **Point to the Zoom button in the Zoom group on the VIEW tab of the Ribbon**
   A ScreenTip appears that describes how the Zoom button works and explains where to find other zoom controls.

2. **Click the Microsoft Word Help (F1) button [?] in the upper-right corner of the title bar**
   The Word Help window opens, as shown in **FIGURE A-15**, displaying the home page for help in Word. Each entry is a hyperlink you can click to open a list of topics. The Help window also includes a toolbar of useful Help commands such as printing and increasing the font size for easier readability, and a Search field. If you are not connected to Office.com, a gold band is displayed telling you that you are not connected. Office. com supplements the help content available on your computer with a wide variety of up-to-date topics, templates, and training. If you are not connected to the Internet, the Help window displays only the help content available on your computer.

3. **Click the Learn Word basics link in the Getting started section of the Word Help window**
   The Word Help window changes, and a list of basic tasks appears below the topic.

4. **If necessary, scroll down until the Choose a template topic fills the Word Help window**
   The topic is displayed in the pane of the Help window, as shown in **FIGURE A-16**. The content in the window explains that you can create a document using a template (a pre-formatted document) or just create a blank document.

5. **Click in the Search online help text box, type Delete, then press [Enter]**
   The Word Help window now displays a list of links to topics about different types of deletions that are possible within Word.

6. **Click the Keep Help on Top button [📌] in the upper-right corner (below the Close button)**
   The Pin Help button rotates so the pin point is pointed towards the bottom of the screen: this allows you to read the Help window while you work on your document.

7. **Click the Word document window, then notice the Help window remains visible**

8. **Click a blank area of the Help window, click [📌] to Unpin Help, click the Close button [✕] in the Help window, then click the Close button [✕] in the upper-right corner of the screen**
   Word closes, and the Excel program window is active.

9. **Click the Close button [✕] to exit Excel, click the Close button [✕] to exit the remaining Excel workbook, click the PowerPoint program button [📧] on the taskbar if necessary, then click the Close button [✕] to exit PowerPoint**
   Excel and PowerPoint both close.

FIGURE A-15: Word Help window

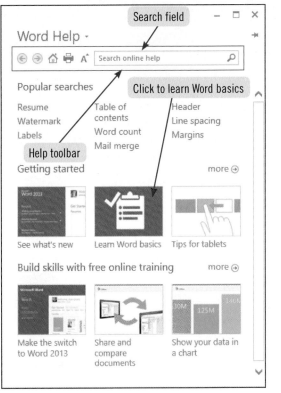

FIGURE A-16: Create a document Help topic

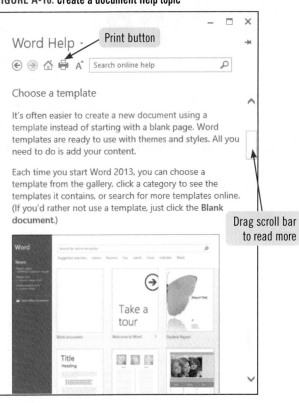

Enabling touch mode

If you are using a touch screen with any of the Office 2013 apps, you can enable the touch mode to give the user interface a more spacious look. Enable touch mode by clicking the Quick Access toolbar list arrow, then clicking Touch/Mouse Mode to select it. Then you'll see the Touch Mode button in the Quick Access toolbar. Click , and you'll see the interface spread out.

Recovering a document

Each Office program has a built-in recovery feature that allows you to open and save files that were open at the time of an interruption such as a power failure. When you restart the program(s) after an interruption, the Document Recovery task pane opens on the left side of your screen displaying both original and recovered versions of the files that were open. If you're not sure which file to open (original or recovered), it's usually better to open the recovered file because it will contain the latest information. You can, however, open and review all versions of the file that were recovered and save the best one. Each file listed in the Document Recovery task pane displays a list arrow with options that allow you to open the file, save it as is, delete it, or show repairs made to it during recovery.

Practice

Concepts Review

Label the elements of the program window shown in FIGURE A-17.

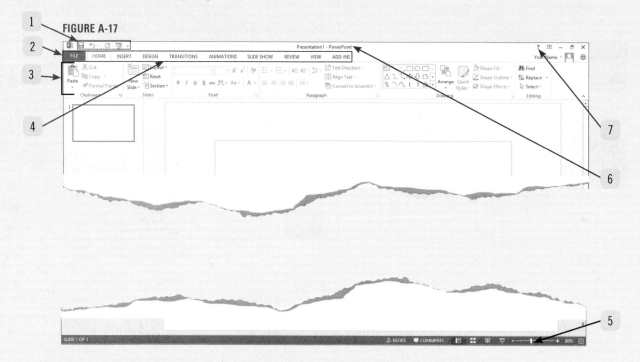

FIGURE A-17

Match each project with the program for which it is best suited.

8. Microsoft Access   a. Corporate convention budget with expense projections

9. Microsoft Excel   b. Presentation for city council meeting

10. Microsoft Word   c. Business cover letter for a job application

11. Microsoft PowerPoint   d. Department store inventory

Independent Challenge 1

You just accepted an administrative position with a local independently owned produce vendor that has recently invested in computers and is now considering purchasing Microsoft Office for the company. You are asked to propose ways Office might help the business. You produce your document in Word.

a. Start Word, create a new Blank document, then save the document as **OF A-Microsoft Office Document** in the location where you store your Data Files.

b. Change the zoom factor to 120%, type **Microsoft Word**, press [Enter] twice, type **Microsoft Excel**, press [Enter] twice, type **Microsoft PowerPoint**, press [Enter] twice, type **Microsoft Access**, press [Enter] twice, then type your name.

c. Click the line beneath each program name, type at least two tasks you can perform using that program (each separated by a comma), then press [Enter].

d. Save the document, then submit your work to your instructor as directed.

e. Exit Word.

Getting Started with Email

CASE ▶ Email is a communication tool that is used for business and personal correspondence. You can use a desktop information management program like Microsoft Outlook 2013, an email program, or any of several Web-based email programs to send and receive email. You are an assistant to Juan Ramirez, the personnel director at Quest Specialty Travel (QST). Juan wants you to learn the basics of email.

Unit Objectives

After completing this unit, you will be able to:

- Communicate with email
- Use email addresses
- Create and send emails
- Understand email folders
- Receive and reply to emails
- Forward emails
- Send email attachments
- Employ good email practices

Files You Will Need

PraguePhoto1.jpg   TopSeven.docx

©theromb/Shutterstock

Communicate with Email

Electronic mail (email) is the technology that lets you send and receive written messages through the Internet. The messages sent using email technology are known as **email messages**, or **email** for short. **Email software**, such as Mail in Microsoft Outlook shown in FIGURE A-1, enables you to send and receive email messages over a computer network. A **computer network** is the hardware and software that enables two or more computers to share information and resources. **CASE** ▶ *Quest Specialty Travel employees use email to communicate with each other and with clients around the world because it is fast, reliable, and easy.*

DETAILS

Email enables you to:

• **Communicate conveniently and efficiently**

Email is an effective way to correspond with coworkers or colleagues. Email can be sent from one person to another person or to a group of people anywhere in the world. You can send and receive messages directly from any computer with an Internet or network connection. You can also send and receive email from wireless devices such as smartphones or tablet computers with email capability. Unlike mail sent using the postal service, email is delivered almost instantaneously. But like mail sent using the postal service, a person receiving an email does not have to be at his or her computer at the same time that a message is sent in order to receive the message.

• **Organize your emails**

You can organize the messages you send and receive in a way that best suits your working style. You can store email messages in folders and refer to them again in the future. Organizing and sorting your saved messages lets you keep a record of communications to manage a project or business. You can also flag messages or you can categorize messages to give an instant visual cue that distinguishes messages that require immediate attention from those that can wait. You can download email to your computer or keep it on the provider's Web server.

• **Send images, video, and computer files as well as text information**

Message text can be formatted so the message is easy to read and appears professional, attractive, or even amusing. Messages can include graphics in the body of the message to convey visual information. See FIGURE A-2. In addition, you can attach files to a message, such as sound or video files, photographs, graphics, spreadsheets, or word-processing documents.

• **Communicate with numerous people at once, and never forget an address**

You can create your own electronic address book that stores the names and email addresses of people with whom you frequently communicate. You can send the same message to more than one person at the same time. You can also create named groups of email addresses, and then send messages to that group of people by entering only the group name.

• **Ensure the delivery of information**

With some email software, you have the option of receiving a delivery confirmation message when a recipient receives your email. In addition, if you are away and unable to access email because of a vacation or other plans, you can set up an automatic message that is delivered to senders so they are alerted to the fact that you might not receive your email for a specified time period.

• **Correspond from a remote place**

If you have an Internet connection and communications software, you can use your computer or handheld device to send and receive messages from any location. If you are using a Web-based email program, such as Outlook.com shown in FIGURE A-3, you can access your email from any computer that is connected to the Internet from anywhere in the world.

FIGURE A-1: Mail window in Microsoft Outlook

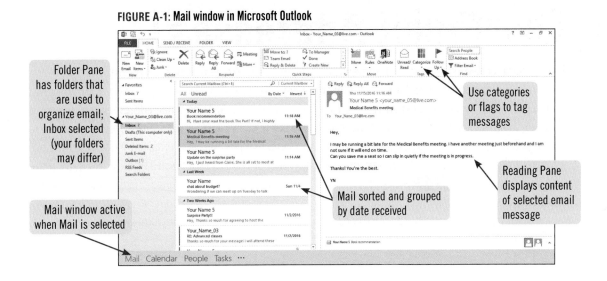

Folder Pane has folders that are used to organize email; Inbox selected (your folders may differ)

Use categories or flags to tag messages

Reading Pane displays content of selected email message

Mail sorted and grouped by date received

Mail window active when Mail is selected

FIGURE A-2: Messages can include formatted text and graphics

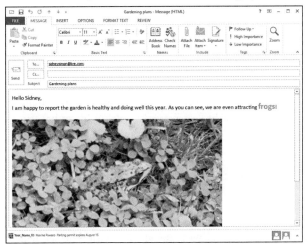

FIGURE A-3: Web-based email Web site Outlook.com

Click to open a new email message window

Use Email Addresses

Learning Outcomes
- Know the four parts of an email address
- Explain the benefits of an email address book

To send and receive email over the Internet using an email program, you must have an email address. Each person has a unique email address. To log in to an email program, a user enters a password in order to send and receive email. To send an email message, you need to know the email address of the person to whom you are sending the message. Instead of having to remember an email address, you can select the name you want from an **address book**, which is a stored list of names and email addresses. In addition, many email programs use an autocomplete feature, which provides a list of email addresses based on the letters as you type. **CASE** *At Quest Specialty Travel, each employee is assigned an email address. As the assistant to the personnel director in the human resources department, you maintain a list of all employee email addresses in an electronic address book. You review the parts of an email address and the benefits of maintaining an email address book.*

DETAILS

An email address has four parts (see FIGURE A-4):

- **Username**

  The first part of an email address is the username. The **username** identifies the person who receives the email. At Quest Specialty Travel, as in many companies, universities, or organizations, usernames are assigned and are based on a specified format. At QST, a username is the first initial of the person's first name and his or her last name. In many email systems, such as those used primarily for personal email, you get to create your username. Username formats can vary based on the requirements of the email service provider, for example, a username might be a person's initial of his or her first name, an underscore, and the last name or it might be a combination of letters and numbers.

- **@ sign**

  The middle part of an email address is the @ sign, called an "at sign." It separates the username from the email service provider. Every email address includes an @ sign.

- **Email service provider**

  The next part of the email address is the email service provider, which actually contains two parts: the service provider and the top-level domain. There are many different service providers. The service provider generally is a company or organization that provides the connection to the Internet and provides email services. The service provider can also be the Web site name for a Web-based email program. The name of the service provider is followed by a dot or period, and then a top-level domain, such as org, com, or edu. Top-level domains help identify the type of service provider. **TABLE A-1** provides some examples of email address formats that are used with different service providers.

The benefits of an email address book include the following:

- **Stores the names and email addresses of people to whom you send email messages**

  Outlook and several other email programs refer to the address book entries as "contacts" and place them in a folder called Contacts. When you create a new contact, you enter the person's full name and email address. You might also have the option to enter additional information about that person, including his or her personal and business mailing address, telephone number, cell phone number, Web page, instant message address, social networking contact information, and even a picture.

- **Reduces errors and makes using email quicker and more convenient**

  Being able to select a contact from your address book not only saves time but also reduces errors. Selecting the email address from an address book reduces the chance that your message will not be delivered because you typed the email address incorrectly. In most email programs, if someone sends you a message, you can add the sender's address as well as other recipients' addresses in the message header directly to your address book without making any errors. **FIGURE A-5** shows a sample address book from Outlook.

FIGURE A-4: Parts of an email address

rdawson@questspecialtytravel.com

© 2014 Cengage Learning

Username At sign Service provider Top-level domain

FIGURE A-5: Outlook 2013 address book with sample contacts

Address Book: Contacts in Your_Name_03@live.com

File   Edit   Tools

Search: ⦿ Name only   ○ More columns   **Address Book**

[   ] Go   Contacts in Your_Name_03@live.com - Your ∨   Advanced Find

Name	Display Name	E-mail Address
Agnes Lee	Agnes Lee (agneslee@live.com)	agneslee@live.com
Benjamin Franklin	Benjamin Franklin (benfranklin@b...	benfranklin@benfranklin.com
Ellen Latsky	Ellen Latsky (elatsky@questspecialt...	elatsky@questspecialtytravel.com
George Washington	George Washington (gwashington...	gwashington@questspecialtytravel...
Jake Ravi	Jake Ravi (jakeravi@live.com)	jakeravi@live.com
Juan Ramirez	Juan Ramirez (jramirez@questspeci...	jramirez@questspecialtytravel.com
Maxine Powers	Maxine Powers (MPowers@questsp...	MPowers@questspecialtytravel.com
Ronald Dawson	Ronald Dawson (rdawson@quests...	rdawson@questspecialtytravel.com
Sidney Simone	Sidney Simone (sidneysimone@live....	sidneysimone@live.com
Your Name	Your Name (yourname@live.com)	yourname@live.com

TABLE A-1: Examples of email providers and addresses

email service provider	examples of email service providers	description of email services	where email is stored	sample email addresses
Corporate or company email	Quest Specialty Travel	Email for employees	On a company server or downloaded to a user's computer	username@ questspecialtytravel.com
Commercial provider: Cable TV, voice, and data communications companies	Comcast Cablevision ATT Verizon	Web space and several email addresses	On an ISP server, until downloaded to a user's computer	username@comcast.net username@optimum.net username@att.net username@verizon.net
Web-based email	Outlook.com (Microsoft) Gmail (Google) Yahoo! Mail (Yahoo!)	Free email addresses and service	On the Web site email server	username@live.com username@gmail.com username@yahoo.com
Educational institution	Wesleyan University University of Delaware	Email for faculty, staff, and students	On the university email server	username@wesleyan.edu username@udel.edu
Organization	American Museum of Natural History	Email for staff	On the organization email server	username@amnh.org

© 2014 Cengage Learning

Create and Send Emails

Learning
Outcomes
• Enter email
addresses in the To
and Cc text boxes
• Write and send an
email message

When you create an email message, you enter the email addresses of the people you want to receive the message in the To or Cc text boxes in the **message header**. You also type a meaningful subject in the **Subject line** so the recipients will have an idea of the message content. You write the text of your message in the **message body**. You can add graphics, format the message text, and attach files. Outlook uses Microsoft Word as the default text editor in email messages, which means that you have access to the same text-formatting features in Outlook that you use when you create Word documents. Most email programs use a basic text editor that enables you to change the color of text, use different fonts, create a bulleted list, and check the spelling of your message. After you create the message, you send it. **CASE** *You write and send a message using Outlook to several employees about an upcoming meeting.*

STEPS

TROUBLE
If this is the first time
that Outlook is being
used, then follow the
on-screen directions
to set up Outlook. If
you are running
Windows 7, click the
Start button on the
taskbar, click All
Programs, click
Microsoft Office
2013, then click
Outlook 2013.

1. **Start Microsoft Outlook 2013, then click Mail on the Navigation Pane in the lower-left corner of the Outlook window if it is not already selected**

   If you are using Outlook, you can start the program and then create a message without connecting to the Internet. If your email program is Web-based, such as Outlook.com, Yahoo! Mail, or Gmail, you have to be connected to the Internet to create an email message. Although you can write and read messages in Outlook and other programs when you are not online, you must be connected to the Internet to send or receive messages.

2. **Click the New Email button in the New group on the HOME tab**

   All email programs provide a button or link that opens a new email window or form so you can begin writing a new message. All email programs have some basic similarities, such as a new message window that provides text boxes or spaces to enter address information, subject, and message content, as shown in **FIGURE A-6**.

3. **Click the To text box, then type the email address of a friend or an associate or you can type your email address**

   Your email message will go to the person at this email address after you send the message. You can send an email message to more than one person at one time; as shown in **FIGURE A-7**, just enter each email address in the To text box and separate the addresses with a semicolon or comma (depending on what your email program requires). You can also click the To button in the message header or the Address Book button in the Names group on the MESSAGE tab to open the Select Names: Contacts dialog box and select each email address from the address book.

QUICK TIP
If your Outlook is set
up with more than
one email account,
you may also see a
From field in the
message header so
you know from
which account you
are sending the
message.

4. **Click the Cc text box, then type another friend's email address**

   Cc stands for carbon or courtesy copy. Courtesy copies are typically sent to message recipients who need to be aware of the correspondence between the sender and the recipients. Bcc, or blind courtesy copy, is used when the sender does not want to reveal who he or she has sent courtesy copies to. Bcc is available in the Select Names: Contacts dialog box.

5. **Click the Subject text box, then type New tour ideas**

   The subject should be a brief statement that indicates the purpose of your message. The subject becomes the title of the message.

6. **Type your message in the message window**

   FIGURE A-7 shows a sample completed message. Many email programs provide a spell-checking program that alerts you to spelling errors in your message. Messages should be concise and polite. If you want to send a lengthy message, consider attaching a file to the message. (You will learn about attaching files later in this unit.)

7. **Click the Send button to send your email message**

   Once the message is sent, the message window closes. Most email programs store a copy of the message in your Sent or Sent Items folder or give you the option to do so.

FIGURE A-6: New message window

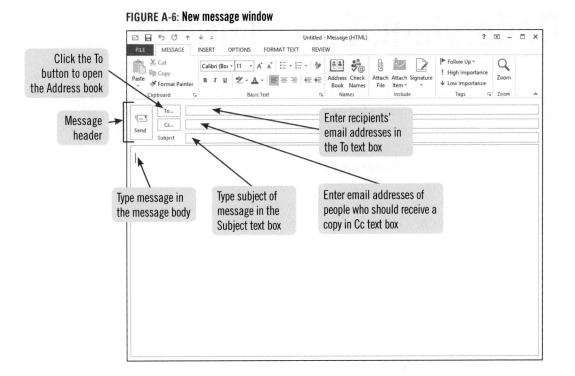

Click the To button to open the Address book

Message header

Enter recipients' email addresses in the To text box

Type message in the message body

Type subject of message in the Subject text box

Enter email addresses of people who should receive a copy in Cc text box

FIGURE A-7: A sample message

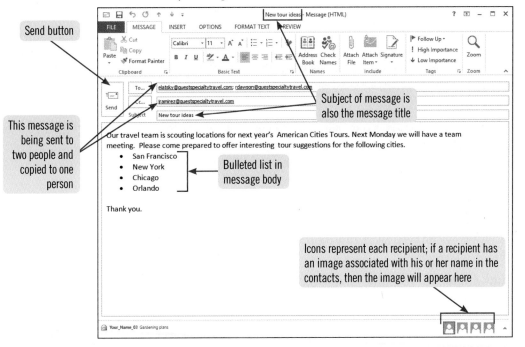

Send button

This message is being sent to two people and copied to one person

Subject of message is also the message title

Bulleted list in message body

Icons represent each recipient; if a recipient has an image associated with his or her name in the contacts, then the image will appear here

Understanding message headers in emails you receive

The message header is the first information that you see when you retrieve your email. The message header contains the basic information about the message. It includes the sender's name and email address, the names and email addresses of recipients and Cc recipients, a date and time stamp, and the subject of the message. Bcc recipients are not shown in the message header. Email programs date- and time-stamp email messages when they are received at the recipient's computer, using the current date and time.

Understand Email Folders

Learning
Outcomes
• Describe the
purpose of each
Outlook default
folder

Just as you save files in folders on your computer, you save email messages in folders in your email program. All email programs provide a way for you to organize and save email messages. You save messages so you can refer to them again in the future. Most email programs come with several default folders. These folders include Inbox, Drafts, Sent Items, Outbox, Deleted Items, and Junk E-mail (or folders with similar names). See **FIGURE A-8**. In addition, you can create additional folders as well as manage folders by using the commands on the FOLDER tab. You can move or copy messages into folders, and you can search messages based on keywords. You can also sort and filter messages within folders to help you find the message you want. **CASE** *As an employee of the QST human resources department, you send and receive lots of messages on several topics. Before organizing your email, you review the default folders in Outlook.*

DETAILS

Most email programs come with default folders, such as the following:

• **Inbox**

An Inbox is a mail folder that receives all incoming email as it arrives. You know who sent the email message because the username or email address and subject line appear in the list of emails in your Inbox, as shown in **FIGURE A-9**. You will also know when the message came in because your computer puts a date on it, which you can see along with the username and subject line. A dark blue bar along the left side of the message info means the message has not been read. A blue highlighted message means the message is selected. If the Reading Pane is open, you can preview the selected message before opening it. You can organize email by date, sender, subject, and other header data by selecting the options at the top of the column.

• **Drafts**

If you want to finish writing a message later, you can save it to the Drafts folder. Many programs automatically save unsent messages at regular intervals in the drafts folder as a safety measure. Depending on how your system is set up, drafts are saved either remotely to a server or locally to your computer.

• **Sent Items**

When you send a message, a copy of it is stored in the Sent Items folder unless you change the default setting. This folder helps you track the messages that you send out. You can change the settings on most email programs so you do not save messages to the Sent Items folder.

• **Deleted Items**

When you delete a message from any folder, it is placed in the Deleted Items folder, sometimes called the Trash folder. The Deleted Items folder keeps items from being immediately and permanently deleted. To empty the Deleted Items folder, click the FOLDER tab on the Ribbon, then click the Empty Folder button in the Clean Up group.

• **Junk E-mail**

Junk email, or **spam**, is unwanted email that arrives from unsolicited sources. Most junk email is advertising or offensive messages. Many email programs have filters that identify this type of email and place it in a special folder. In Outlook, this folder is called Junk E-mail. This makes it easy for you to delete the email you don't want. It is possible that a message that you do want might get caught by the spam filter. It is good practice to look at the headers in the Junk E-mail folder before deleting the messages stored there.

• **Outbox**

The Outbox is a temporary storage folder for messages that have not been sent. If you are working offline or if you set your email program so messages do not get sent immediately after you click the Send button, the messages are placed in the Outbox. When you connect to the Internet or click the Send/Receive All Folders button in the Send & Receive group on the SEND/RECEIVE tab, the messages in the Outbox are sent.

FIGURE A-8: Default mail folders

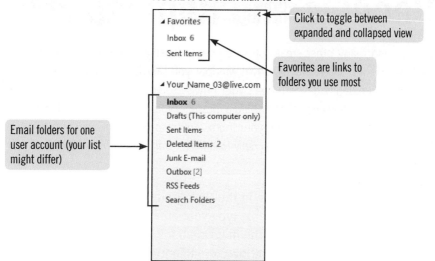

Click to toggle between expanded and collapsed view

Favorites are links to folders you use most

Email folders for one user account (your list might differ)

FIGURE A-9: Outlook Mail window

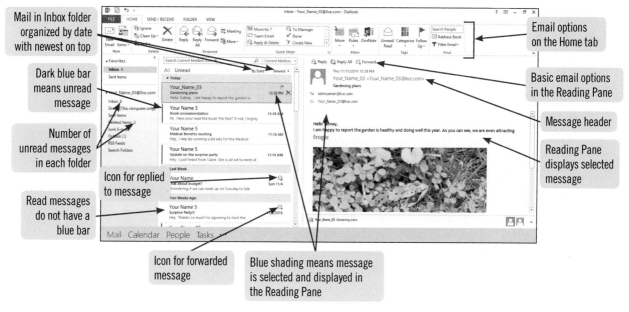

Mail in Inbox folder organized by date with newest on top

Dark blue bar means unread message

Number of unread messages in each folder

Icon for replied to message

Read messages do not have a blue bar

Icon for forwarded message

Blue shading means message is selected and displayed in the Reading Pane

Email options on the Home tab

Basic email options in the Reading Pane

Message header

Reading Pane displays selected message

Managing your email

You would be surprised at how quickly your Inbox, Sent Items, and Deleted Items folders can fill up. How can you manage these? The best way is to create folders for specific projects or people that you know will create a high volume of email. For example, if you are working on a special project, create a folder for that project. And, since folders can be nested, you can create folders within the main folder to continue to organize emails related to the project. The FOLDER tab provides many commands to help you manage your email. To create a new mail folder, click the FOLDER tab, click the New Folder button in the New group to open the Create New Folder dialog box, type the new folder name, select the folder you want to place the new folder in, then click OK. Any email that you receive or send about the project can be moved into that folder.

Depending on your email program, you can also categorize, flag, or label messages. You can sort email by any message header, such as date, subject, flag or label, or sender to find an important message quickly. Create a Search folder to display messages that are flagged or that meet certain criteria, such as from a certain person. Search folders display but do not store messages. Once the project is completed, you can archive or delete that folder's email using the buttons in the Clean Up group on the FOLDER tab. Email takes up storage space, and if you are running out of storage on your computer, your email is a good place to start cleaning up the hard drive, especially the Sent Items, Junk, Junk E-mail, and Deleted Items folders.

Receive and Reply to Emails

Learning
Outcomes
• Send, receive,
  view, and reply to
  an email message

Outlook and many other email software programs let you preview a selected message in the Reading Pane. To open the message in its own window, you can double-click the message header. The default in Outlook is to hide images to protect your privacy so you might have to click a link or button to display inserted graphics or video. After reading a message, you can reply to it, delete it, move it to another folder, flag it for follow-up, or keep it in your Inbox. You respond to the sender of the message by clicking the Reply button. **CASE** *You often reply to email messages from the QST staff and from clients.*

STEPS

1. **Click the New Email button in the New group on the HOME tab to open a new message window, click the To text box, type your email address, click the Subject text box, type Practice using email, click the message body text box, then type I am sending this message to myself to learn how to send and reply to messages.**

TROUBLE
You might have to wait a few moments before the email message comes in.

2. **Click the Send button in the message window, click the SEND/RECEIVE tab, click the Send/Receive All Folders button in the Send & Receive group, click the Sent Items folder to verify that the message was sent, then click the Inbox folder**

   Clicking Send sends the message out unless you have changed the default setting to place the message in the Outbox but not send it. Clicking the Send/Receive All Folders or Send All buttons tells your email program to send messages in the Outbox and to deliver incoming messages to your Inbox. Many email programs deliver email to your Inbox when you sign in with your username and password. Outlook plays an alert tune and displays the unread message in the Inbox with a blue bar on the left side.

QUICK TIP
Outlook may display the message header in a pop-up window if you are using another program when the message arrives.

3. **Click the Practice using email message in the Inbox to select it and view the message**

   You read the message header to identify the message by subject, date, and sender. The selected message appears in the Reading Pane in the Outlook window.

4. **Double-click the Practice using email message in the center pane to open it**

   See **FIGURE A-10**. The Message window has several options. Reply lets you reply to the original sender. The Reply All option lets you reply to the original sender and all the Cc recipients of the original message. Bcc recipients are not included in Reply or Reply All messages. The Quick Steps group offers commands frequently used to manage email.

5. **Click the FILE tab, then click Close**

   The email message window closes, and you return to the Outlook window. The Practice using email message is still selected.

QUICK TIP
You can also click the Reply button in the Reading Pane.

6. **Click the HOME tab, then click the Reply button in the Respond group**

   Clicking the Reply button automatically opened a message addressed to the original sender in the Reading Pane. The subject line is preceded by "RE:", indicating that the message is a reply. The header from the original message appears above the original message. The insertion point is at the top of the message body. The COMPOSE TOOLS MESSAGE tab is active.

7. **Type This is my reply to my original message. in the message body**

   It is helpful to include the original message in a reply to help the message recipient recall the topic. Outlook saves a draft of your message automatically. See **FIGURE A-11**. Depending on how you set up your email program, you can automatically include or exclude the text of the original sender's message, including the message header and body.

8. **Click the Send button in the Reading Pane**

   The message is sent, and a copy of it is stored in your Sent Items folder. Most email programs add a Replied to Message icon 🔁 next to the original message in the Inbox, indicating that you have replied to the message.

FIGURE A-10: Message open in new window

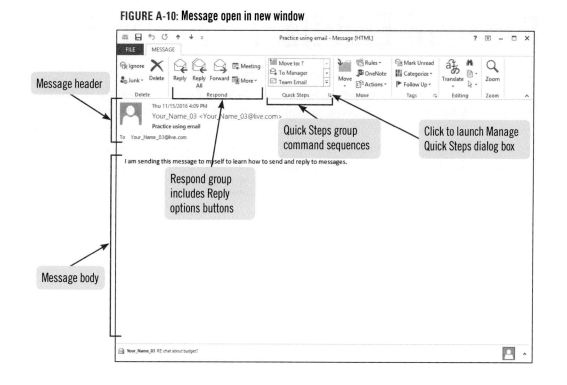

Message header

Quick Steps group command sequences

Click to launch Manage Quick Steps dialog box

Respond group includes Reply options buttons

Message body

FIGURE A-11: Replying to a message

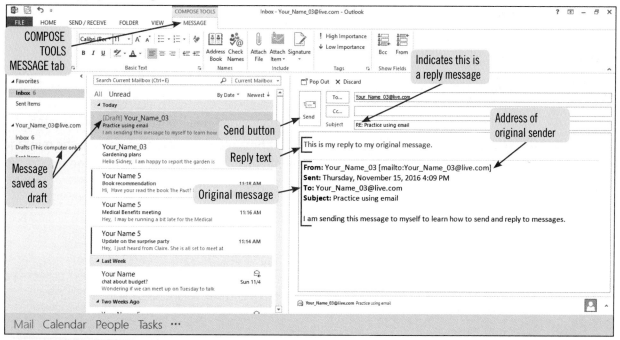

COMPOSE TOOLS MESSAGE tab

Send button

Reply text

Message saved as draft

Original message

Indicates this is a reply message

Address of original sender

Mail   Calendar   People   Tasks   ···

Setting up vacation responses

Most email programs allow you to set up an automatic response or vacation message if you are not going to be able to receive your email for a specified period of time. This is a helpful way to let people know that you are not ignoring any email they send, but rather that you are not reading your email. When vacation mode is active, your email program automatically sends out a reply when a message comes in. You determine the content of the reply message. A typical message might be "Thank you for your message. I am on vacation from July 1 to July 10 and will respond to your message when I return." Most email programs only send one automatic response to each sender each day or within a specified period of time.

Outlook 2013

Forward Emails

You might receive an email that you need to send to someone else. Sending a message you have received from one person to someone else is called **forwarding**. When you forward a message, you send it to people who have not already received it—that is, people not in the To or Cc text boxes of the original message. You can include an additional message about the forwarded message in the message body. The subject of the forwarded message is preceded by FW:, but the subject stays the same so you can organize it by subject as a conversation with any other messages on the same topic. In most email programs, you forward a message that you have received to another person by clicking the Forward button. **CASE** *As an assistant in the human resources department at QST, you sometimes get email from clients that you forward to the travel agents at their branch offices.*

STEPS

1. **Click the SEND/RECEIVE tab, then click the Send/Receive All Folders button**

   Outlook sends messages in the Outbox and delivers any incoming messages to your Inbox.

2. **Click the HOME tab, click the Inbox, then click the newest Practice using email message in the center pane if it is not selected**

   You read the message header to identify the message. You can see the original recipients of the message by reviewing the header. You can see who received the message by reviewing the email addresses in the To and Cc areas of the header (if there were courtesy copies). You will not know who might have received a Bcc on the message. When you view a message, you see buttons in the Reading Pane that provide several options for responding to the message. One of the options is to click the Forward button to forward the message.

3. **Click the Forward button in the Reading Pane**

   A New Message window opens in the Reading Pane. Clicking the Forward button does not automatically address the email to anyone; the To, Cc, and Bcc address fields are blank. The entire original message is included in the body of the message. The subject line is preceded by "FW:", indicating that the message is a forwarded one. Most email software includes the message header from the original message in the Message window above the original message. The insertion point is at the top of the message window in the To field. You can address this message as you would any new email and include multiple Cc and Bcc recipients.

4. **Type a friend's email address in the To text box, place the insertion point in the message body above the forwarded message, then type I am forwarding this message to you as a test for class. Please let me know you received it. as shown in FIGURE A-12**

   If you have Contacts in your address book, you can click the To button to open the Select Names: Contacts dialog box and click to select the email address for your recipients. You can also click the Address book button in the Names group on the MESSAGE tab to open the Select Names: Contacts dialog box.

5. **Click the Send button in the message window**

   The message is sent, and a copy of it is stored in your Sent Items folder. Most email programs add a Forwarded Message icon next to the original message, indicating that you have forwarded the message.

Controlling your message

When you communicate with email, take extra care in what you say and how you say it. The recipient of an email message cannot see body language or hear the tone of voice to interpret the meaning of the message. For example, using all capital letters in the text of a message is the email equivalent of shouting and is not appropriate. Carefully consider the content of a message before you send it, and don't send confidential or sensitive material. Remember, once you send a message, you might not be able to prevent it from being delivered. Email is not private; you cannot control who might read the message once it has been sent. Do not write anything in an email that you would not write on a postcard that you send through the postal service. If your email account is a company account, be sure you know the policy on whether or not your company permits the sending of personal messages. All messages you send through an employer's email system legally belong to the company for which you work, so don't assume that your messages are private.

FIGURE A-12: Forwarding a message

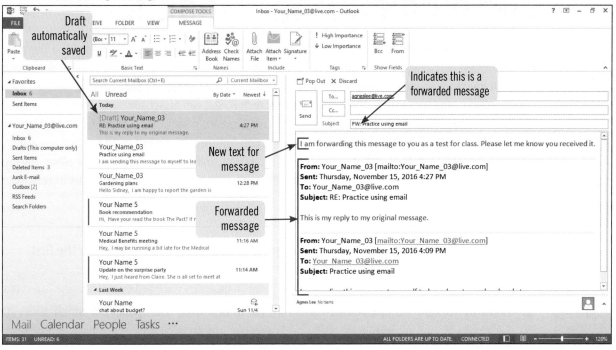

Flagging or labeling messages

Most email programs provide a way to identify or categorize email. If you use email for business, school, or personal communication, you will find that you receive many email messages. Some can be read and discarded. Others require additional attention or follow-up. Organizing your email can help you keep up with the many messages you are likely to receive. If you are using Outlook, flags can assist you in your effort to manage your email. If you click the flag icon next to the message, it is marked by default with a red Quick Flag. However, you can use flags of different shades of red to mark messages for different categories of

follow-up. To apply a flag, click the flag in the message you want to flag. To select from a list of flag actions and specify a due date, right-click a message, then click Add Reminder to open the Custom dialog box.

Outlook also allows you to color-code messages for categories. See **FIGURE A-13**. If you are using Web-based email, you might have other options for categorizing, labeling, or flagging email. For example, Gmail provides a way to assign a label to email or to star email for easy sorting or organizing.

FIGURE A-13: Flagging and using colors to categorize messages

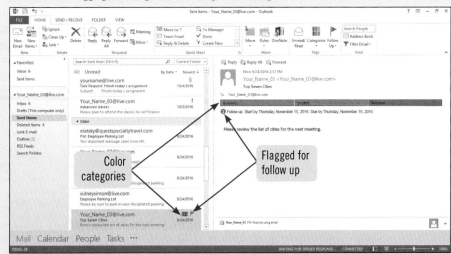

Send Email Attachments

In addition to composing a message by typing in the Message window, you can attach a file to an email message. For example, in an office environment, employees can attach Word or Excel documents to email messages so other employees can open them, make changes to them, and then return them to the original sender or forward them to others for review. You can attach any type of computer file to an email message, including pictures, video, and audio. Keep in mind that to open an **attachment** created using a particular software program, the recipient of the attachment will need that software to open the attached file. **CASE** *You often send trip photos from clients to people in the office. You also have to send documents to employees throughout the year. Attaching files is a common task in your job in the human resources department.*

STEPS

1. **Click the New Email button in the New group on the HOME tab, then type the first three letters of your email address in the To text box**

   Notice as you start to type, a list of email addresses based on the letters you typed opens under the To text box.

2. **Point to the address you want to enter in the To text box, then click your email address**

   The email address you clicked is entered in the To text box. You can send a message with an attachment to more than one person at one time; just enter each email address in the To text box, separated by a semicolon or comma. You can also click the Cc text box or Bcc text box, and then enter email addresses for recipients who are to receive a Cc or Bcc.

3. **Click the Subject text box, type Top Seven Cities, click the message body, then type Please review the list of cities for the next meeting.**

4. **Click the Attach File button in the Include group on the MESSAGE tab**

   The Insert File dialog box opens, as shown in **FIGURE A-14**. The name of the command or way to access the dialog box might differ slightly, but most email programs provide a way to attach files, either with an Attach link or with an Attach a File or Attach button. You might have to click a Browse button to navigate to the file or files you want to attach. Often you can use the icons or Thumbnails view in the dialog box to see what the files look like before you attach them to a message.

5. **Navigate to the location where you store your Data Files, click TopSeven.docx, then click Insert**

   Once attached, files appear in the Attached text box, as shown in **FIGURE A-15**. Often, an icon next to each filename indicates the type of file it is. The numbers in parentheses next to the filenames specify the size of each file. Most programs will allow you to attach more than one file to a message. Some Internet service providers will limit message size or the number of attachments for one email. Attachments such as movies might be too large for some email systems to handle. As a general rule, try to keep the total size of attachments below 1 MB. Also, consider the Internet connection speed of the recipient's computer. If a recipient does not have a fast Internet connection, a large file could take a long time to download.

6. **Click the Send button to send the message**

FIGURE A-14: Attaching a file in Outlook

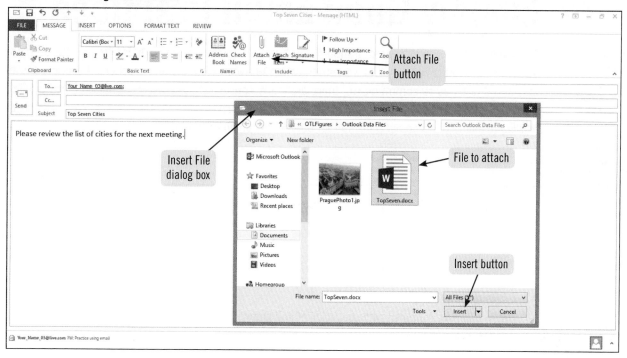

FIGURE A-15: Message with attached file

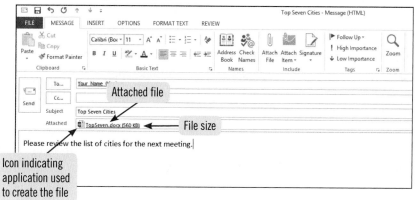

Reviewing options when sending messages

Email programs can have several options that affect how messages are delivered. To change these message options in Outlook, click the OPTIONS tab in a Message window to view the Message Options, then click the launcher in the More Options group to open the Properties dialog box shown in **FIGURE A-16**. You can, for example, assign a level of importance and a level of sensitivity so the reader can prioritize messages. You can also encrypt the message for privacy. If both the sender and recipient are using Outlook, you can add Voting buttons to your message for recipients to use when replying. In addition, when you want to know when a message has been received or read, you can select the Request a delivery receipt for this message check box or the Request a read receipt for this message check box. You can also specify a future date for delivering a message if the timing of the message is important.

FIGURE A-16: Message options

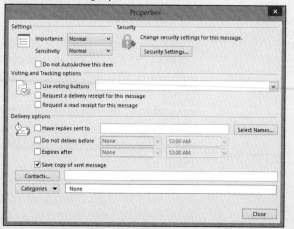

Employ Good Email Practices

Email has become an accepted standard for business correspondence. It is also widely used for personal communication as well as communication between students and teachers. Although it is an easy and a fast way to communicate, there are many considerations to keep in mind before sending email. **CASE** ▶ *Working in the human resources department, you are responsible for corporate policy relating to email. You send out a memo that outlines the company policy for email.*

DETAILS

The following are good practices to follow when sending and receiving email:

- **Be considerate**

  Always be polite and use proper spelling and grammar in email messages. Be sure to use the spelling checker as a last step before sending messages.

- **Consider file size**

  Unless you have consulted with the recipient and know that he or she can receive large file attachments, avoid sending any attachment that exceeds 1 MB.

- **Be safe**

  Never open an email message unless you know who sent it to you. Keep your spam filter, spyware software, and virus software up to date. Be sure to run the virus checker through all emails you receive. Keeping computers safe from viruses and spyware is very important.

- **Think before forwarding**

  Before you forward a message, consider the contents of the message and the privacy of the person who sent the message. A joke, a story, or anything that is not personal usually can be forwarded without invading the sender's privacy. When you are certain the sender would not mind having his or her message forwarded, you can forward the message to others.

- **Be professional**

  In very casual correspondence, you can present an informal message by using shortcuts like "LOL" for "laughing out loud" and "BRB!" for "be right back!" However, limit this technique to personal messages. Any email that is intended for professional use or is a reflection on a professional organization should not use shortcuts.

- **Limit emoticons**

  You can use **emoticons** in your text to show how you are feeling. You create an emoticon by combining more than one keyboard character to make a graphic. For example, type a colon and a closing parenthesis to make a smiley face.

- **Maintain your account**

  Outlook offers Clean Up tools, as shown in **FIGURE A-17**. Most programs offer similar tools for maintaining your folders. When you are finished using an email program, it is good practice to delete or archive email messages that you no longer need. If working for a company, you should comply with corporate policy. For personal email, you should periodically delete unneeded messages from the Sent Items to help manage storage space on your computer. It is also good practice to empty the Deleted Items folder. To delete a message, first you select it. Then you can do one of the following: click the Delete button in the Delete group on the HOME tab, press the [Delete] key, or click the Delete button ✕ to the right of the message when you mouse over it. To empty the Deleted Items folder, right-click the folder, then click Empty Folder, Empty Trash, or Empty Deleted Items folder. You can also click the FOLDER tab, then click the Empty Folder button in the Clean Up group. When you see a confirmation message, as shown in **FIGURE A-18**, click Yes.

FIGURE A-17: The Clean Up tools

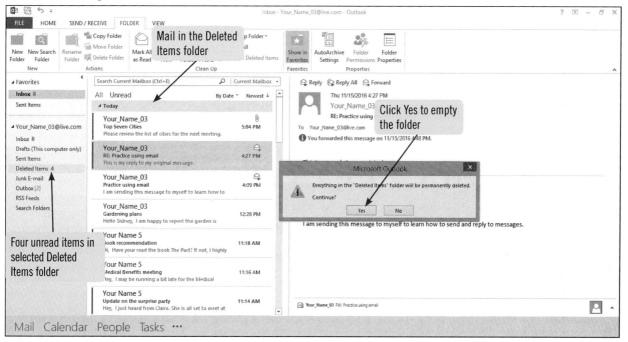

FIGURE A-18: Deleting items

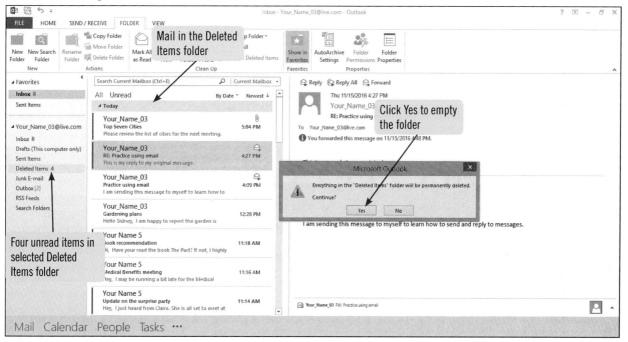

Creating distribution lists

When using an email program to communicate with friends or coworkers, you might find that you need to send messages to the same group of people on a regular basis. If your address book contains many contacts, it can take time to scroll through all the names to select the ones you want and you might forget to include someone in an important message. Fortunately, email programs provide an easy way to group your contacts. You can create a **distribution list**, or a **contact group**, which is a collection of contacts to whom you want to send the same messages. Distribution lists, or contact groups, make it possible for you to send a message to the same group of email addresses without having to select each contact in the group. For example, if you send messages reminding your human resources staff of a weekly meeting, you can create a distribution list called "HR-STAFF" that contains the names and email addresses of your staff who must attend the meeting. When you want to send a message to everyone on the team, you simply select HR-STAFF from the address book, instead of selecting each person's name individually. Once you create a distribution list, you can add new members to it or delete members from it as necessary. If you change information about a contact that is part of a group or list, the list is automatically updated.

Practice

Concepts Review

Label each element of the Message window shown in FIGURE A-19.

FIGURE A-19

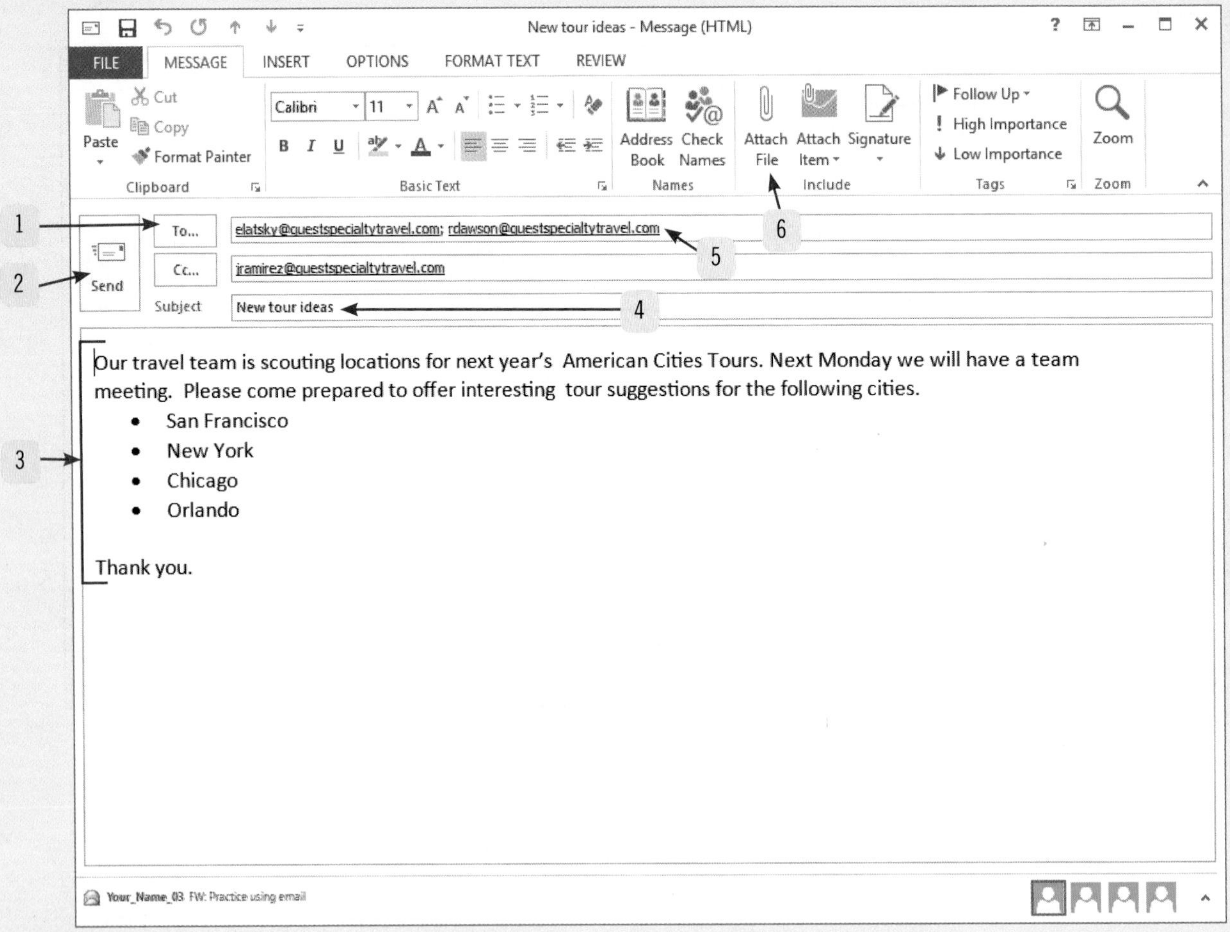

Match each term with the statement that best describes it.

7. **Drafts folder**

8. **Attachment**

9. **Bcc feature**

10. **Your_Name@live.com**

11. **Inbox**

12. **RE:**

a. Folder that receives arriving email

b. An email address

c. File sent with an email

d. Identifies a replied to message

e. Contains messages you are creating but haven't sent yet

f. Hides email address of recipient to all others

Select the best answer from the list of choices.

13. When you can't view or respond to email messages right away, you should set up a(n) _____ to alert people who send an email message that you are not currently available.
    - **a.** Contact list
    - **b.** Delivery option
    - **c.** Vacation response
    - **d.** Alias

14. Unless you have consulted with the recipient and know that he or she can receive large file attachments, avoid sending any attachment that exceeds _____.
    - **a.** 30 MB.
    - **b.** 30 GB.
    - **c.** 1 MB.
    - **d.** 1 GB.

15. Files you send along with your email messages are called _____ and can be of any file type, such as documents, spreadsheets, video, images, and sound files.
    - **a.** Attachments
    - **b.** Headers
    - **c.** Drafts
    - **d.** First three lines of the message body

16. If you do not want the recipients of your message to see the others you also sent the message to, you should use the _____ feature.
    - **a.** Cc
    - **b.** Flag
    - **c.** Outbox
    - **d.** Bcc

17. An email that you are still working on is stored in the:
    - **a.** Inbox.
    - **b.** New Mail folder.
    - **c.** Drafts folder.
    - **d.** Sent Items folder.

18. When you forward a selected message to another person, the email addresses for the original recipients of the message:
    - **a.** Appear only in the To text box in the message header.
    - **b.** Do not appear in any text box in the message header.
    - **c.** Appear only in the Cc text box in the message header.
    - **d.** Appear in the To and the Cc text boxes in the message header.

19. To ensure that you send the same message to the same group of multiple recipients, set up a(n):
    - **a.** Address book.
    - **b.** Quick Step.
    - **c.** Draft folder.
    - **d.** Contact group or distribution list.

20. The _____ features help you follow up and organize messages.
    - **a.** Attach files and folders
    - **b.** Cc and Bcc
    - **c.** Flag and categorize
    - **d.** FW and RE

Skills Review

Note: To complete this Skills Review, your computer must be connected to the Internet.

1. **Communicate with email.**
   a. Start Outlook.
   b. Click Mail if it is not selected.
   c. Click the Send/Receive All Folders button to get new email delivered to the Inbox.
   d. Open the Inbox to view any new messages.

2. **Use email addresses.**
   a. Open a new message window.
   b. Click the To text box, then type your **email address**.
   c. Type a friend's **email address** in the Cc text box.

3. **Create and send emails.**
   a. Type **Employee Parking Lot** as the subject of the message.
   b. Place the insertion point in the message body, type **Please be sure to park in your designated parking spot. Thank you.**
   c. Send the message.

Skills Review (continued)

4. **Understand email folders.**

   a. Review the mail folders in your email program.

   b. Look in the Sent Items folder for the Employee Parking Lot message.

   c. Open the Deleted Items folder. See if any email is in that folder.

   d. Review the Spam or Junk E-mail folder.

5. **Receive and reply to emails.**

   a. Click the Send/Receive All Folders button to deliver messages to your Inbox.

   b. Display the contents of the Inbox folder.

   c. Read the message from yourself.

   d. Click the Reply All button.

   e. Place the insertion point in the message body, type **Where can I get my parking permit?**, then send the message.

6. **Forward emails.**

   a. Forward the message you received to another friend.

   b. Place the insertion point in the top of the forwarded message body, type **This important message came from HR.** See **FIGURE A-20**.

FIGURE A-20

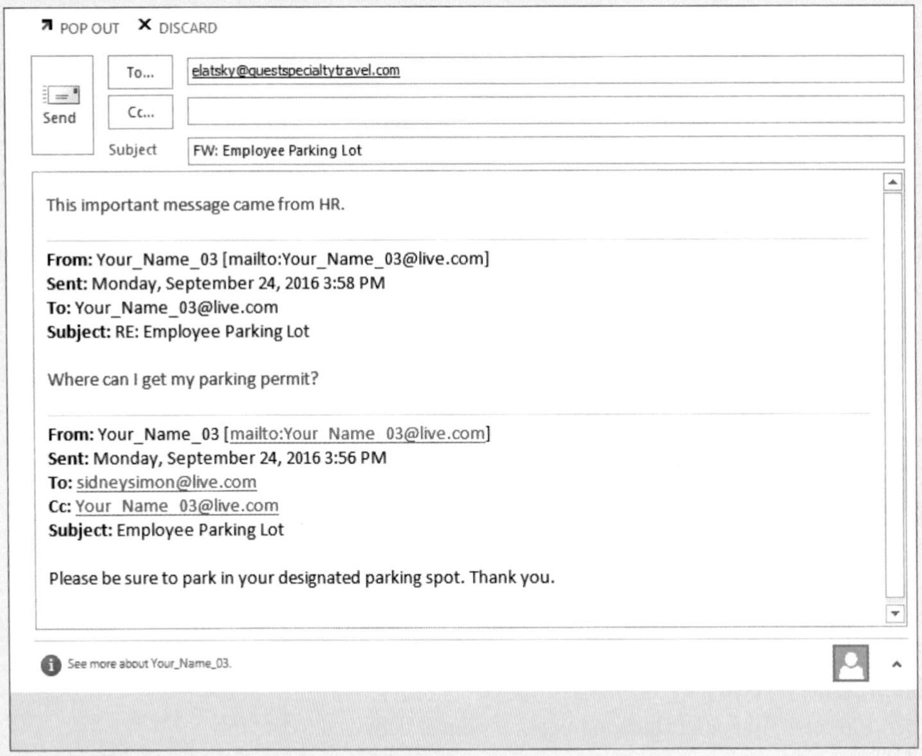

   c. Send the message.

   d. Close the original message if you opened it in a new window.

7. **Send email attachments.**

   a. Create a new email message.

   b. Enter your **email address** as the message recipient.

   c. Enter a friend's **email address** in the Cc text box.

   d. Enter **Travel photo** as the subject of the message.

   e. In the message body, type **Here is the photo from my trip to Prague.**

Skills Review (continued)

f. Click the Attach File button in the Include group on the MESSAGE tab.

g. Navigate to the location where you store your Data Files.

h. Select the file **PraguePhoto1.jpg**, then click Insert. See **FIGURE A-21**.

FIGURE A-21

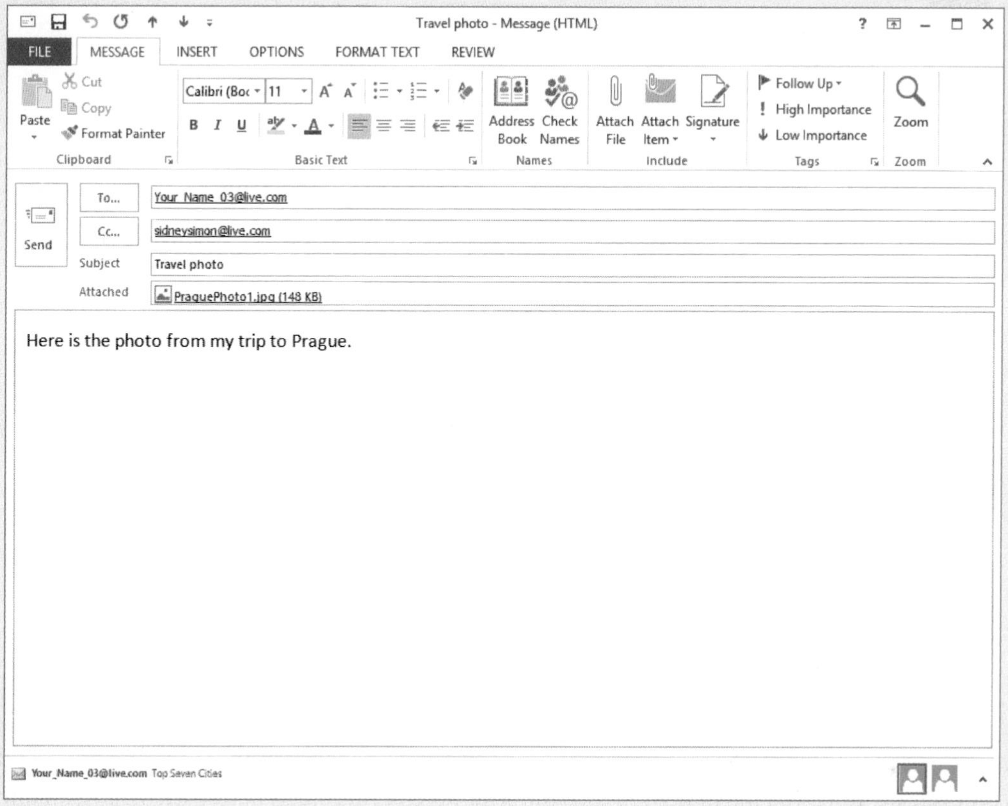

i. Send the message.

8. Delete items.

a. Delete all of the messages received in this exercise from the Inbox folder.

b. Delete all of the messages sent in this exercise from the Sent Items.

c. Empty the Deleted Items folder.

d. Exit Outlook.

Independent Challenge 1

You have been appointed to chair the committee to bring a farmer's market to town. You decide to use email to communicate with the other members of the committee as well as the town council and the mayor. *Note: To complete the Independent Challenge, your computer must be connected to the Internet.*

a. Start Outlook.

b. Create a new message, and address it to yourself, then use the Cc field to send this message to two other people. Use the names and email addresses of classmates, teachers, or friends.

c. Type **Farmer's Market** as the subject of the message.

d. In the message body, type **There will be a public hearing on Thursday evening to meet with representatives of Local Growers Inc. We should prepare our presentation and contact the local newspaper to be sure they cover the story.**

Independent Challenge 1 (continued)

e. Press [Enter] two times, then type your name. See **FIGURE A-22**.

f. Send the message, then click the Send/Receive All Folders button. Depending on the speed and type of Internet connection you are using, you might need to click the Send/Receive All Folders button again, after waiting a few moments, if you do not receive the email in your Inbox the first time you click the Send/Receive All Folders button.

g. Open the message in the Inbox, flag it with a follow-up flag, then print it.

h. Forward the message to another person you did not include in the original mailing.

i. In the message body, type **Forgot to include you in this mailing! Please read the message; hope you can be there.**

j. Send the message.

k. Delete all of the messages related to this Independent Challenge from the Inbox folder. Delete all of the messages related to this Independent Challenge from the Sent Items.

l. Empty the Deleted Items folder.

m. Exit Outlook.

Independent Challenge 2: Explore

You are planning a vacation with a group of friends. Think about a trip you would like to take, and consider this destination as you work on this Independent Challenge. You have to send email messages with an attachment as you organize this trip. *Note: To complete the Independent Challenge, your computer must be connected to the Internet.*

a. Start Outlook, then create a new message and address it to two contacts, such as friends, family members, or classmates.

b. Enter your email address in the Cc text box.

c. Type **Our vacation plans** in the Subject text box.

Independent Challenge 2: Explore (continued)

d. Start your word processor, and write a brief letter to your friends to encourage them to join you on the adventure. Briefly detail your plans and reasons for selecting the destination. For example, if you are planning a trip to Gettysburg, Pennsylvania, you might explain that you want to learn more about Abraham Lincoln. If you are planning a trip to Orlando, Florida, you can say how much fun it is to go to theme parks. Save the document file to the location where you store your Data Files, using a filename you will remember.

e. Type a short note in the message body of the email to the recipients of the message, telling them you thought they would like to join you on this trip and you are looking forward to them coming along.

f. Attach the document you created in your word processing program to the message.

g. Send the message, then click the Send/Receive All Folders button. Depending on the speed and type of Internet connection you are using, you might need to click the Send/Receive All Folders button again, after waiting a few moments, if you do not receive a response email the first time you click the Send/Receive All Folders button.

h. Print a copy of the message you receive in response.

i. Connect to the Internet, then using a browser and your favorite search engine locate a picture or graphic image that you want to send through email.

j. Right-click the picture, then click E-mail picture on the shortcut menu. (Alternatively, after right-clicking a picture, you might see other options, but sending the picture through email will be one option even though the exact wording for the E-mail picture option might be different depending on your software and system.)

k. Click Allow if asked to go outside the protected zone, click OK if a dialog box opens asking if you want to make the picture smaller.

l. Click Attach to attach the image to a new message window if prompted. (*Note:* A new message window will open titled Emailing: images, or, if the new window does not open automatically, click the Outlook icon on the taskbar.)

m. Enter your email address in the To text box, then add Cc and Bcc recipients. (*Note:* To open the Bcc text box, click the Cc button.) The subject will be filled in automatically. Write a brief message in the body of the message. Set a priority level. Use **FIGURE A-23** as a guide.

n. Send the message, then read the message, and view the picture when it arrives in your Inbox.

o. Delete all of the messages received for this Independent Challenge from your Inbox.

p. Delete all of the messages sent for this Independent Challenge from the Sent Items.

q. Empty the Deleted Items folder.

r. Exit Outlook.

FIGURE A-23

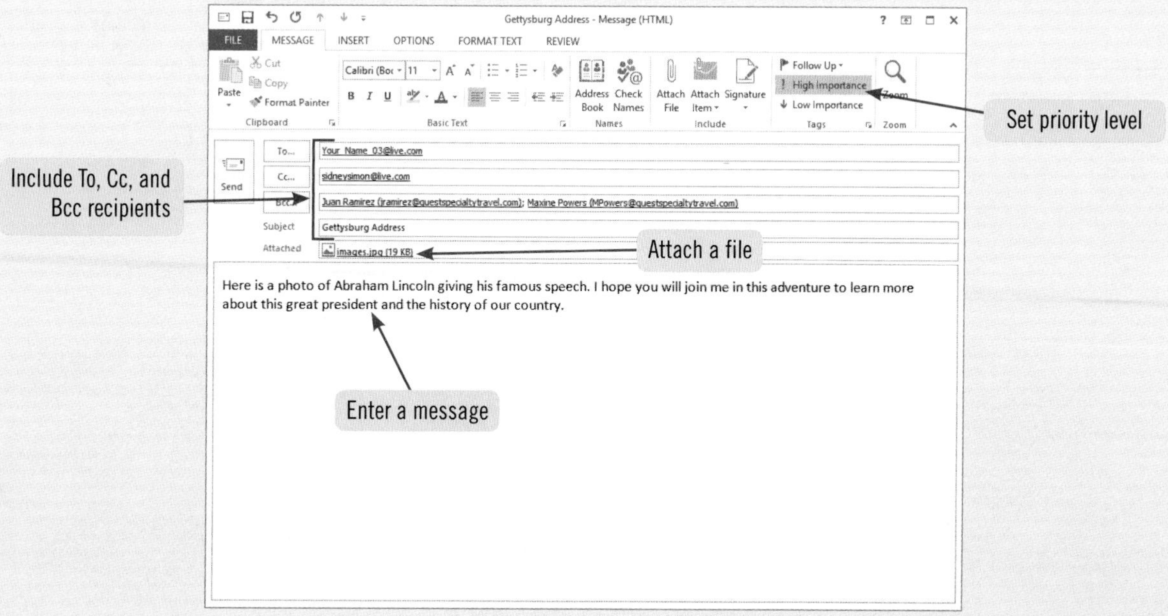

Visual Workshop

Refer to the email message in **FIGURE A-24** to complete this Visual Workshop. Use Outlook to create and then send this message. Be sure to send the message to at least one recipient. Attach a file that you created on your computer. It can be a document, worksheet, image, or database file. *Note: To complete the Visual Workshop, your computer must be connected to the Internet.*

FIGURE A-24

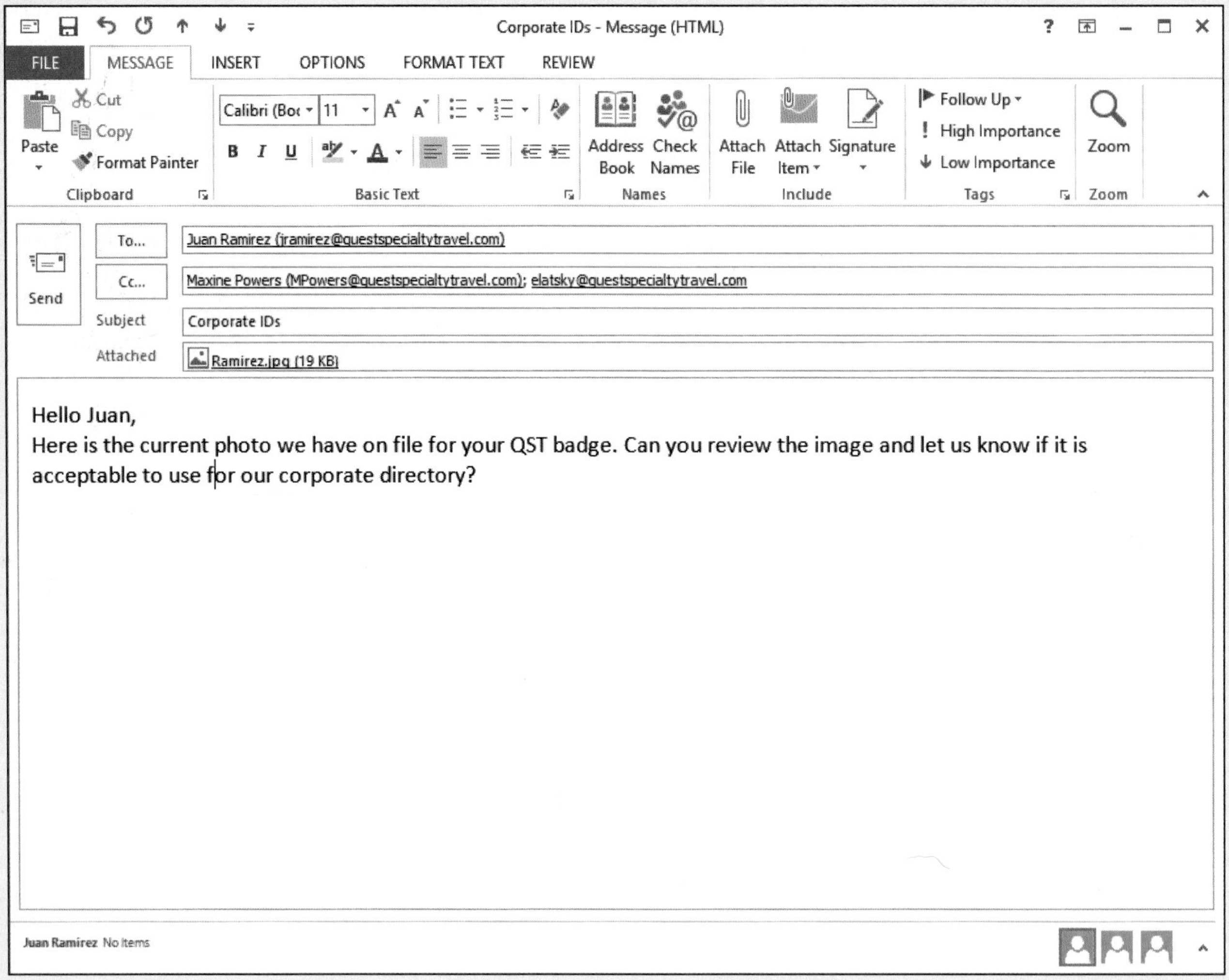
Corporate IDs - Message (HTML)
FILE
MESSAGE
INSERT
OPTIONS
FORMAT TEXT
REVIEW
Cut
Copy
Paste
Format Painter
Clipboard
Basic Text
Address Book
Check Names
Names
Attach File
Attach Item
Signature
Include
Follow Up
High Importance
Low Importance
Tags
Zoom
To...
Juan Ramirez (jramirez@questspecialtytravel.com)
Cc...
Maxine Powers (MPowers@questspecialtytravel.com); elatsky@questspecialtytravel.com
Send
Subject
Corporate IDs
Attached
Ramirez.jpg (19 KB)
Hello Juan,
Here is the current photo we have on file for your QST badge. Can you review the image and let us know if it is acceptable to use for our corporate directory?
Juan Ramirez No Items

Managing Information Using Outlook

CASE Outlook is a complete personal information and time management program you can use for all your business and personal data. Outlook integrates Mail, Calendar, People, Tasks, and Notes modules that let you manage your mail, appointments and activities, contacts and address book, to-do list, and notes all in one program.

Unit Objectives

After completing this unit, you will be able to:

- Describe Outlook
- Organize email
- Manage your contacts
- Manage your calendar

- Manage tasks
- Create notes
- Integrate social connectors
- Apply categories

Files You Will Need

No files needed.

©theromb/Shutterstock

Describe Outlook

Learning Outcomes
• Explore the Outlook modules
• Create customized views

The Outlook screen is fully customizable to let you personalize how you view and get to the information about the people you interact with, your appointments and schedule, or mail, with different levels of detail. The first time you start Outlook, you will be prompted to set up a **personal account** that identifies you as a user. If you want to use Outlook for email, you must set up your email account. You can set up more than one account in a single installation of Outlook. Each account requires a username and password. **CASE** *As the assistant to Juan Ramirez in the human resources department, you learn Outlook so you can use it for communication and scheduling.*

STEPS

1. **Start** Microsoft Outlook 2013

   Mail is the default starting module for Outlook. You use the **Navigation Pane** by clicking the Calendar, People, or Tasks buttons to switch between modules. When Mail is selected, the upper part of the Navigation Pane shows the Folder List, which can be minimized or expanded. The information on the status bar varies depending on which module is active. When Mail is active, the status bar includes the number of messages in the Inbox, the mail server connection status, and zoom percentage of the window.

2. **Click the** VIEW **tab on the Ribbon, click the** Message Preview **button in the Arrangement group, then click** 1 Line **even if it is already checked**

   The options on the VIEW tab let you customize each view in Outlook. The Message Preview option determines how many lines of each email in the center pane you see, which helps you review your messages.

3. **Click the** To-Do Bar **button in the Layout group, click** Calendar, **click the** To-Do Bar **button, click** Tasks, **click the** Reading Pane **button, then click** Right

   The To-Do Bar, which opens on the right side of the window, includes the Date Navigator (calendar) and tasks (including appointments). The **Date Navigator** gives you an overview of the month.

4. **Click the** HOME **tab on the Ribbon, click an** email message **in the center pane, click the** VIEW **tab, click the** People Pane **button in the People Pane group, then click** Normal

   The People Pane opens at the bottom of the Reading Pane. The People Pane shows social media information available for any people who were included in the header of the message in the Reading Pane, as well as attachments, appointments, and notes related to those people. See **FIGURE B-1**.

5. **Click the** HOME **tab, click the** More button ⊽ **in the Quick Steps group, review the menu that opens, then click anywhere outside the menu to close the Quick Steps menu**

   Quick Steps are shortcuts that help you complete basic Outlook tasks with one click.

6. **Click each button in the Navigation Pane:** Calendar 📅, People 👥, **and** Tasks ☑, **reviewing each window as it opens**

   Mail, Calendar, People, and Tasks are all modules in Outlook. As you place the mouse on each button, a Peek appears showing you a brief view window into the module. The Mail button is ✉.

7. **Click** ••• **in the Navigation Pane, click** Notes, **review the window that opens, click** •••, **click** Folders, **then review the pane that opens**

   The Folder Pane in Folders view shows you the folders for storing your email, calendar, and contacts.

8. **Click** •••, **click** Navigation Options, **then click the** Compact Navigation check box **to remove the check mark if there is one**

   FIGURE B-2 shows the Navigation Options dialog box. You can customize the Navigation Pane to your personal preferences. The Navigation Pane can be compact or expanded.

9. **Click** OK, **then click** Mail

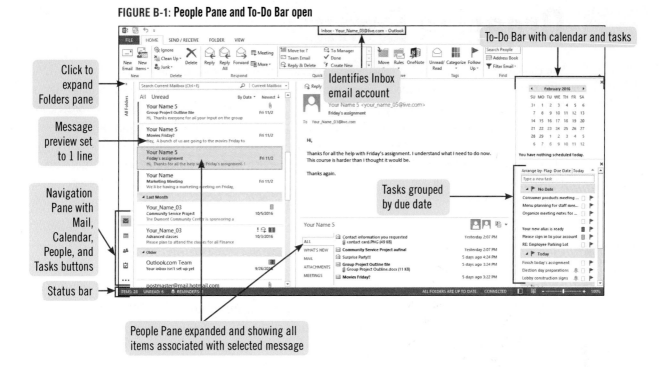

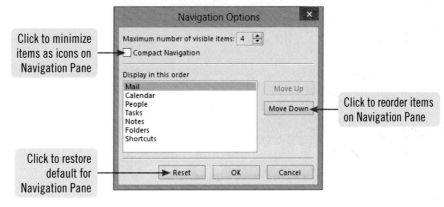

Weather in Calendar view

What you do during a day may change depending on the local weather. You cannot ski if there's no snow, and a trip to the beach can be disrupted by thunderstorms. When you display the Calendar module, weather information for the next 3 days is displayed above the calendar. The weather location is the default city for the account in which Outlook was installed. This city name appears to the left of the weather information. To change the weather location displayed, click the arrow next to the city name in Calendar view, then click Add Location from the menu. You can type a city name, country, or zip code, and then select from the suggested list. To customize the Weather options, click the FILE tab, click Options, click Calendar, scroll down to Weather, click the Show weather on the calendar check box to turn the feature on or off, then click the Show temperature in: Celsius or Fahrenheit option button. Weather settings are saved for each user profile, and you must be connected to the Internet for this feature to work.

Organize Email

You can create and send email using any email program; most essential features are the same across the programs. If you use Outlook Mail as your email program, you can use it to organize your email, such as by conversation, view, or folder. By default, Outlook groups the mail by date, and **sorts**, or orders, the email in descending order by date received. You can use the People module to store your email addresses as contacts, see relevant contact information when email arrives, and get meeting requests through email. These requests then become appointments on your Calendar. You can search messages for specific content, dates, or senders. All new email arrives in the Inbox folder unless you set up rules to deliver email to other folders. A **rule** is an action you can create to have Outlook automatically handle messages in a certain way. **CASE** ▷ *You will receive email from clients and QST employees. You set up Outlook to view and manage the email using its many organizational features.*

STEPS

1. **Click Mail in the Navigation Pane, click the Inbox in the Folder Pane, click the VIEW tab on the Ribbon, click the To-Do Bar button in the Layout group, click Off, click the People Pane button in the People Pane group, then click Off**

   The **Mail module** is the active module. The People Pane and the To-Do Bar are closed. See **FIGURE B-3**. A list of all mail folders is in the Folder Pane, divided into sections. The Favorites section at the top of the Folder Pane is available for you to create shortcuts to folders you use most often. The Mail Folders section under the Favorites section contains the folders associated with each user account. It includes the default mail folders discussed in Unit A and any folders the user has created. When you click a folder in the Folder Pane, the contents of the folder appears in the center pane. Color-coding and icons associated with the messages in the center pane help you identify mail that is read, unread, has been forwarded or replied to, or has attachments. You can move your mouse pointer over a message in the center pane for additional options, such as a delete button or Follow-Up flags for messages.

2. **Click the Arrange By button in the center pane**

   The menu opens as shown in **FIGURE B-4**. You see the many ways of filtering, sorting, grouping, and arranging email messages. If you show the messages as **conversations**, all emails that discuss a common subject or thread will be grouped together. The Subject of a message defines the conversation. **Message threading** allows you to navigate through a group of messages, seeing all replies and forwards from all recipients about a particular topic. You can search your messages using keywords.

3. **Click the FILE tab on the Ribbon, verify that Info is selected in the Navigation Pane, click the Manage Rules & Alerts button, then click the New Rule button**

   The Rules and Alerts dialog box opens, and then the Rules Wizard opens, as shown in **FIGURE B-5**. You can specify how you want your mail from specific senders—or other criteria—to be sorted as it arrives. The Rules Wizard provides templates to help you create rules. The rules help you **filter** your email messages based on specific criteria, such as who sent you a message.

4. **Click Cancel to close the Rules Wizard, click Cancel to close the Rules and Alerts dialog box, click Options in the Navigation Pane, then click Mail in the left pane of the Outlook Options dialog box**

   Mail options set up the way you compose, send, receive, organize, track, view, save, and format messages.

5. **Scroll through the list of options, click Cancel, click the HOME tab, then click the Junk button in the Delete group**

   By specifying safe senders (Never Block Sender) and blocked senders (Block Sender), you can be sure that the email you get is the email you want to receive.

6. **Click the Inbox for your account in the Folder Pane, click the VIEW tab, click the Reset View button in the Current View group, then click Yes if a warning message opens**

   You can control how the email appears in any folder by using the View options.

FIGURE B-3: Mail in Outlook

Four unread messages in the Inbox; Inbox selected

Unread messages

Selected message included two courtesy copies

Default mail folders

Status bar provides up-to-date information about Inbox

Replied message icon

Email message coded with three color categories

Message with attachment icon

Envelope icon in Outlook button on taskbar indicates new mail in Inbox

Envelope icon on taskbar indicates new mail in Inbox

FIGURE B-4: Arrange By options

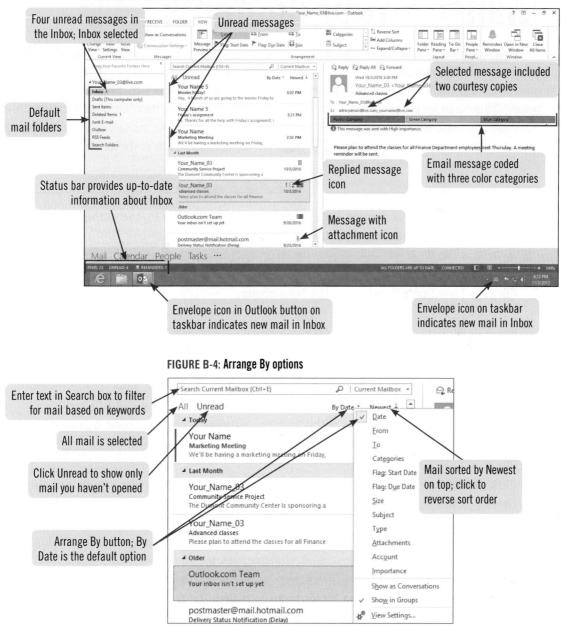

Enter text in Search box to filter for mail based on keywords

All mail is selected

Click Unread to show only mail you haven't opened

Arrange By button; By Date is the default option

Mail sorted by Newest on top; click to reverse sort order

FIGURE B-5: Setting up Rules and Alerts

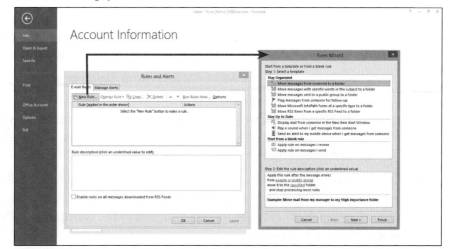

Manage Your Contacts

Learning Outcomes
- Explain how fields are used to define contacts
- Enter data to create a new contact

The **People module** in Microsoft Outlook lets you manage all your business and personal contact information. When you enter the information for a contact, you store general and detailed data about that person. Once you have added a person's social networking contact information, you can view that contact's social network updates if they've added you as a friend, if they are in your circle of friends, or if they have a public profile. Once you create a contact, you can quickly address letters, locate a phone number, make a call, send a meeting request, assign a task, or email a message. **CASE** *You learn about Contacts so you can store all the contact information for employees and clients in Outlook.*

STEPS

1. **Click People in the Navigation Pane, click the HOME tab, click Phone in the Current View group, then click People in the Current View group**

   Outlook displays the People module using the People view, which shows several contacts in the Contacts folder. See **FIGURE B-6**. The other options in the Current View group let you view contacts in different ways.

> **QUICK TIP**
> Click the File as list arrow in the Contact window, then click one of the options in the list to identify how Outlook files each contact.

2. **Click the New Contact button in the New group**

   A new, untitled contact card opens. You enter information for a new contact in each field. A **field** is an area that stores one piece of information. If you do not enter a first and last name in the Full Name text box, the Check Full Name dialog box opens so you can enter the full name for the contact.

> **TROUBLE**
> If the This is the mailing address check box is checked, deselect it.

3. **Type your name as the contact name in the Full Name text box, press [Tab], type Quest Specialty Travel (QST) in the Company text box, press [Tab], type Human Resources Assistant Manager in the Job title text box, type your email address, type www.questspecialtytravel.com as the Web page address, type telephone numbers in the appropriate text boxes, click the Addresses Business arrow, click Home, then enter your home address**

> **TROUBLE**
> If you don't want to reveal personal information, enter any made-up data for your card.

4. **Click the Addresses Home list arrow, click Business, click the This is the mailing address check box to select it, type 55 Orange Avenue in the Address text box, then click the Business Fax field**

   If Outlook can't identify an address component that you type in the Address text box, the Check Address dialog box opens for you to verify the component. You can store up to three addresses in the Address text box. You choose Business, Home, or Other from the Addresses list, then type the address in the Address text box.

> **QUICK TIP**
> Click the Normal or Reading View buttons on the status bar to change the view. Use the Zoom slider to increase or decrease the size and number of cards that fit on a screen.

5. **Type 55 Orange Avenue in the Street text box, select the text in the City text box, type Chicago, select the text in the State/Province text box, type IL, press [Tab], type 60600, then click OK**

   The completed contact card should look similar to **FIGURE B-7**.

6. **Click the Save & Close button in the Actions group, click Business Card in the Current View group, click Card in the Current View group, then double-click the contact with your name to open the CONTACT tab with information for that contact**

7. **Click the Picture icon to open the Add Contact Picture dialog box**

   The information on any card can be changed, and new data added at any time for any contact.

8. **Add a photo of yourself or click Cancel, then click the Details button in the Show group**

   You can enter more detailed information about the contact. Any birthday or anniversary dates entered in the contact card will appear on the Calendar as a recurring event.

9. **Click the Birthday calendar icon 🗓, click today's date on the calendar that opens, click the Save & Close button in the Actions group, click the Business Card button in the Current View group, then click the Calendar button in the Navigation Pane**

   Your birthday appears in the Calendar.

FIGURE B-6: Contacts in People module

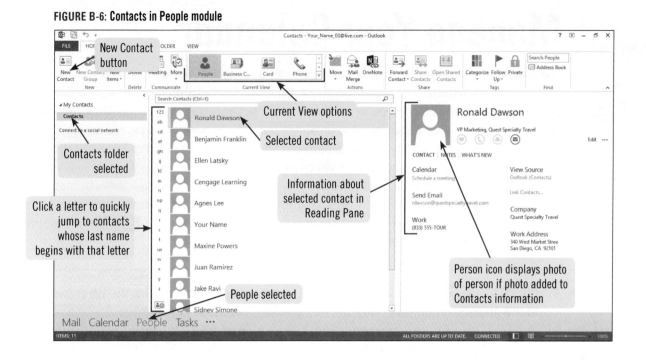

FIGURE B-7: Completed new Contact card

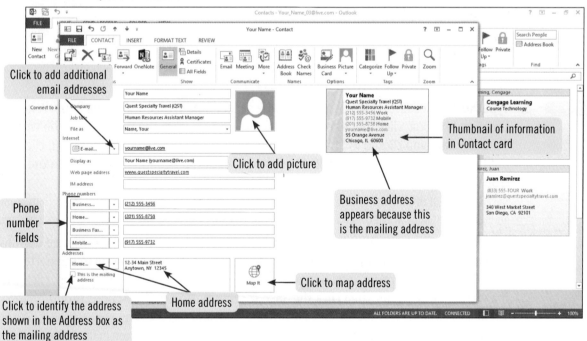

Manage Your Calendar

Learning
Outcomes
• Describe the features of Calendar
• Create a recurring appointment

The **Calendar module** in Microsoft Outlook provides a convenient, effective way to manage your appointments and remember events. See FIGURE B-8. Outlook defines an **appointment** as an activity that does not involve inviting other people or scheduling resources, a **meeting** as an activity you invite people to or reserve resources for, and an **event** as an activity that lasts 24 hours or longer. You can specify the subject and location of an activity and its start and end times. Outlook can sound and display a reminder for you before the start of the activity. When you create an activity, Outlook notifies you if the new activity conflicts with, or is adjacent to, another scheduled activity. You can set up recurring activities by specifying the recurrence parameters, such as every week, month, or any period of time, and specify when the recurrence ends. People in your group or company can each have their own calendars. **CASE** > *You will use Outlook to manage the schedule for the human resources department.*

STEPS

TROUBLE
If more than one calendar is open, and appear side-by-side, remove the check marks to close all but your calendar.

1. **Click Calendar in the Navigation Pane if it is not already selected, click the Week button in the Arrange group, then click the Month button in the Arrange group**

   The calendar can be viewed either by day, work week, week, or month. The Folder Pane, if open, shows the current and next month in the Date Navigator. You can click the arrows in the Date Navigator to move forward or backward month by month, or you can click the month to select from a list. Dates with appointments or events appear in bold in the Date Navigator. You click the Next Appointment button or Previous Appointment button if no appointment appears in the current time period to view your appointments. If you place the pointer on any activity, the **Peek** feature opens to show details, including reminder notices and the recurring icon for recurring events.

2. **Click any date next week in your calendar, click the HOME tab if it is not selected, then click the New Appointment button in the New Group**

   An untitled Appointment window opens. You use this window to specify the subject, location, reminders, and start and end times of an event. You can choose how you want to display your time associated with a scheduled appointment, such as Busy or Out of Office. You can add meeting notes and invite other people who are connected to your calendar. You can even categorize the appointment with a color.

QUICK TIP
To see upcoming tasks using the Calendar, click the VIEW tab, click the To-Do Bar button, then click Tasks.

3. **Type Human Resources meeting in the Subject text box, type Conference Room A in the Location text box, click the Start time calendar icon 🔳, click the date that is one week from the date you clicked in Step 2, click the Start time list arrow, click 9:00 AM, click the End time list arrow, click 10:00 AM (1 hour), click the Reminder list arrow in the Options group, then click 1 day**

   See FIGURE B-9. If this was a one-time meeting, you could click the Save & Close button in the Actions group and the appointment would be set. However, since this is a monthly meeting, you set a recurrence pattern.

4. **Click the Recurrence button in the Options group, review the default recurrence options shown in FIGURE B-10, click the Monthly option button, notice the change in the patterns, click the End after option button, type 12 in the occurrences text box, click OK, click OK if a warning box opens, then click the Save & Close button in the Actions group**

   The Appointment window closes. This is a recurring appointment that will be displayed on your calendar each month for a year. Recurring events or appointments appear with the 🔁 icon in the Peek window.

QUICK TIP
To quickly enter an appointment, click the time slot in the calendar, then type the information.

5. **Click any date the week before the scheduled appointment, click the HOME tab, click the Day button in the Arrange group, click the Work Week button, click the Week button, then click the Forward button ▶ in the calendar three times**

   You can view the calendar by day, week, or month. In all calendar views, you can click the Time Scale button in the Arrangement group on the VIEW tab to change the level of detail of the days shown.

6. **On the HOME tab, click the Today button in the Go To group to return to today's date**

FIGURE B-8: Calendar for a month

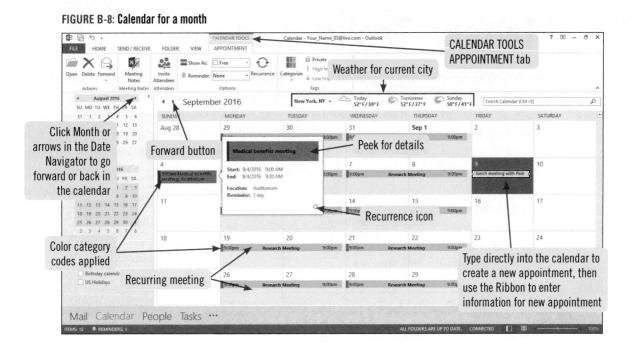

FIGURE B-9: New Appointment window

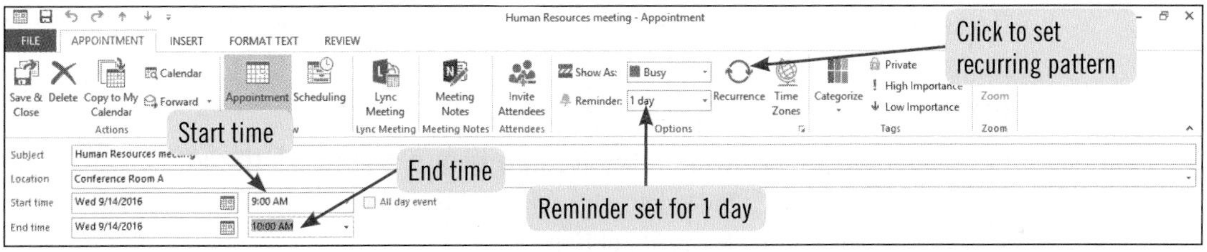

FIGURE B-10: Appointment Recurrence dialog box

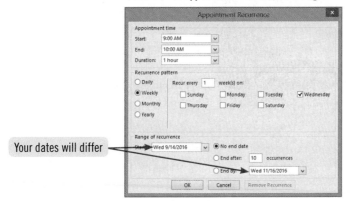

Sending electronic business cards

You can send contact information over the Internet easily with Outlook. If you know someone has Outlook, you can send a contact business card. In People view, click the contact you want to send, then, on the HOME tab, click the Forward Contact button in the Share group. You can choose to send the card as a business card or an Outlook contact. If you send it as a business card, you will send the contact as a .vcf electronic file to someone via email.

Manage Tasks

Learning Outcomes
• Explain the features of the Tasks module
• Create a new Task and set the Date, Priority, and Reminder fields

Tasks in Outlook are an electronic to-do list. When you have something you need to do, you can enter it in the **Tasks module**. Each task has a subject, a start and due date, and a description. You can also assign a priority to a task. You can mark your progress on tasks by percentage complete, and you can have Outlook create status summary reports in email messages and then send the summary to anyone on a task update list. Tasks can also have reminders. If you **flag** an email message, it appears as a task in your task list to remind you to follow-up. When you are in an Outlook module other than Tasks, your tasks appear at the bottom of the To-Do Bar if it is open. You can also view the tasks that are due on each date in the Calendar. Similar to meetings and events, tasks can recur. You can also assign a flag and category to each task to help you organize your tasks. **CASE** ▸ *A month from today, the lobby of the office is getting new tile. You have to make sure the employees use the back entrance by setting up signs before the job begins. You enter the task in Outlook to keep track of it.*

STEPS

1. **Click Tasks in the Navigation Pane, then click the New Task button in the New group**
   The new untitled Task window opens.

2. **Type Lobby construction permit in the Subject text box, click the Follow Up button in the Tags group, click Flag Message, click the Start calendar icon 🔳, click the date that is one month from today, click the Priority list arrow, click High, click the Reminder check box to select it, click the Reminder calendar icon 🔳, then click the date that is three weeks from today**
   The completed task looks like **FIGURE B-11**.

3. **Click the Save & Close button in the Actions group, then click the VIEW tab**
   FIGURE B-12 shows Tasks as a To-Do List with a ScreenTip (a Peek) displaying additional task information about one task. A few existing tasks appear in the window (your screen will be different).

4. **Click the Change View button in the Current View group**
   A gallery opens with different options for viewing tasks. You can also sort and group tasks using the options in the Arrangement group on the VIEW tab, including by Category, Start Date, Due Date, Folder, Type, or Importance. Click the Reverse Sort button in the Arrangement group to change sort order.

5. **Click the HOME tab, click the New Task button in the New group to open the Untitled Task window, then click the Assign Task button in the Manage Task group**
   You can assign tasks to another person and have Outlook automatically update you on the status of the task completion. To assign a task, you fill in the email address of the person to whom you are assigning the task, complete the task details, and then click Send.

6. **Click the To text box, type your friend's email address, click the Subject text box, type Organize meeting notes for HR in the Subject text box, click the Status arrow, click In Progress as shown in FIGURE B-13, then click the Send button in the message window**
   The task you created appears in the To-Do List for No Date. You may need to scroll down to see the task. Notice the task icon has a person icon with an arrow to indicate this task is assigned to another person.

7. **Click Calendar in the Navigation Pane, click the Today button in the Go To group if the calendar does not open to today, then place the pointer over Tasks in the Navigation Pane to see the tasks list**

8. **Click the VIEW tab, click the To-Do Bar button in the Layout group, then click Tasks**
   To schedule time to complete a task, you drag a task from the To-Do Bar to a time block in the Calendar.

FIGURE B-11: Task information entered

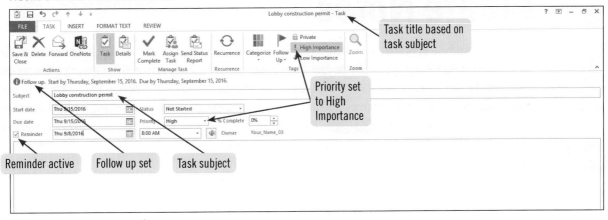

FIGURE B-12: Tasks in To-Do List view

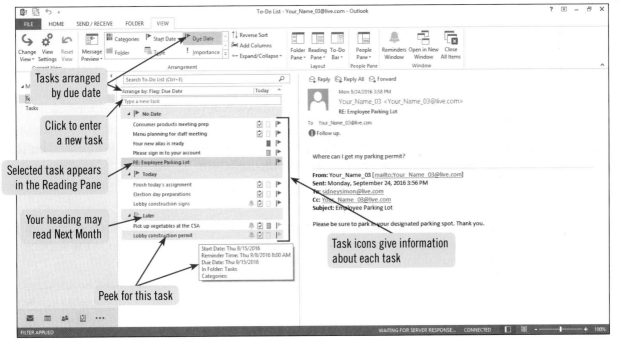

FIGURE B-13: Assigning a task

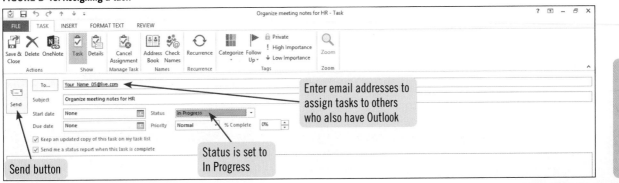

Create Notes

Learning
Outcomes
• Create a new Note
  in Outlook
• Create an event
  from a note

The **Notes module** in Microsoft Outlook provides access to notes, which are the electronic version of the sticky notes or Post-It notes you buy at your local stationery store. Notes created in Outlook are a convenient way to quickly jot down a reminder or an idea. You can group and organize notes, like tasks and appointments, and you can assign categories, contacts, or colors to them. You can also forward a note to share an idea with a colleague. **CASE** *You use the Notes module in Outlook to quickly write down an idea concerning a new employee at Quest Specialty Travel.*

STEPS

TROUBLE
If the new note fills
the screen, double-
click the title bar to
create a thumbnail
version of the note.

1. **Click ⋯ in the Navigation Pane, click Notes on the menu, then click the New Note button in the New group on the HOME tab**

   A blank new Note opens. See **FIGURE B-14**. You type your note directly in the Note window, which is a separate window that you can move by dragging the title bar. The icon in the upper-left corner of the note opens a menu. The note should begin with a meaningful phrase so the Notes list displays a clear descriptive title for it.

2. **Type Maxine Powers - Parking permit expires August 15, then click the Note Close button ☒**

   The note appears in the Notes window.

QUICK TIP
If a note is covering
an area of the
window you want to
view, click the title bar
of the note and drag
it to a new location.

3. **Click the New Note button, type Order coffee for kitchen, then click the Note Close button ☒**

   All new notes appear next to any existing notes that have been created previously. See **FIGURE B-15**. Notes are date- and time-stamped at the time they are created.

4. **Drag the Maxine Powers- Parking permit expires August 15 note to the Calendar button on the Navigation Pane, then release the mouse button**

   A new Appointment window opens with the details from the note entered in the Subject line and the notes area.

5. **Click the Start time calendar icon 🖩, click August 15 for the next year, click the All day event check box, refer to FIGURE B-16, then click the Save & Close button in the Actions group**

   You now have an event to remind you about the contents in the note. In a similar way, you can drag a note to the Tasks button in the Navigation Pane to create a task based on the note. When you drag a note to the Tasks button, a new task window opens so you can specify a due date and other details for the task.

QUICK TIP
To quickly copy a
note, drag the note
while you press [Ctrl].

6. **Right-click a note to open the shortcut menu, review the options on the menu, then press [ESC]**

   You can use the shortcut menu to copy, print, forward, or delete notes. In addition, the Current View group on the HOME tab and the VIEW tab provide many options for viewing notes so you can organize them the way you want.

FIGURE B-14: New note

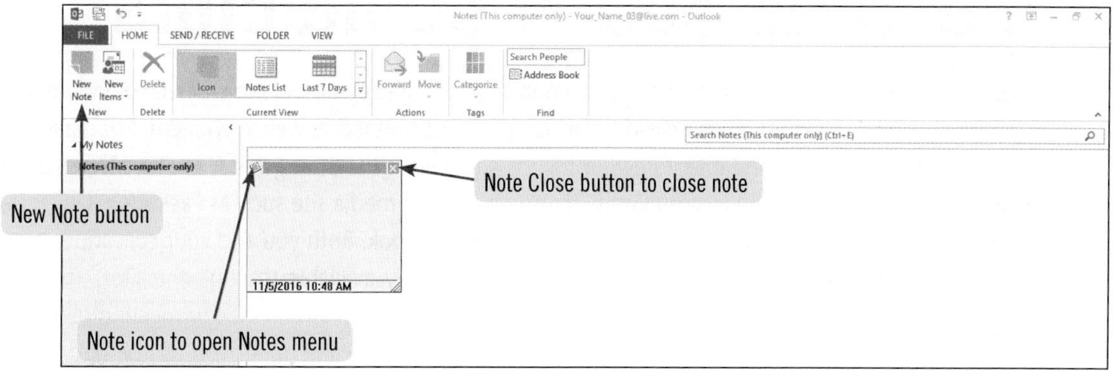

New Note button

Note icon to open Notes menu

Note Close button to close note

11/5/2016 10:48 AM

FIGURE B-15: Two completed notes

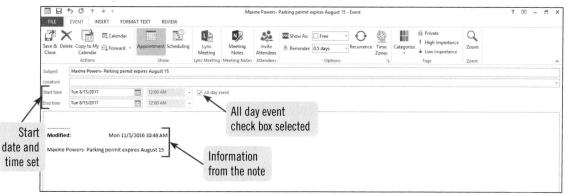

Icon view is the current view

Completed notes in Icon view

Maxine Powers- Parking permit expires August 15

Order coffee for kitchen

FIGURE B-16: Creating an event from a note

Maxine Powers- Parking permit expires August 15 - Event

Subject: Maxine Powers- Parking permit expires August 15

Location:

Start time: Tue 8/15/2017 12:00 AM ☑ All day event
End time: Tue 8/15/2017 12:00 AM

All day event check box selected

Start date and time set

Modified: Mon 11/5/2016 10:48 AM

Maxine Powers- Parking permit expires August 15

Information from the note

Customizing Outlook Today

Outlook Today is an Outlook feature that lets you view your Calendar, Tasks, and Messages for the day. To open Outlook Today, click ••• in the Navigation Pane, click the Shortcuts button on the menu, then click Outlook Today in the left navigation pane. Outlook Today is divided into three panes: Calendar, Tasks, and Messages. The Calendar pane shows your appointments. The Tasks pane shows your tasks, which you can sort in Outlook Today by Importance, Due Date, Creation Time, or Start Date and in ascending or descending order. If you use Outlook for email, the Messages pane displays how many messages are in your Inbox, Drafts, and Outbox folders.

To customize Outlook Today, click the Customize Outlook Today link to the right of the date in Outlook Today, and set the options to fit your personal style and work habits. In the Customize Outlook Today pane, you can decide to go directly to Outlook Today when Outlook opens if it does not open automatically, and pick a different visual appearance for Outlook Today from an available list, among other options. When you are finished customizing your settings, be sure to click the Save Changes link in the upper-right corner of the Customize Outlook Today pane to save any changes you make.

Integrate Social Connectors

Learning
Outcomes
• Describe how to
link Outlook to
social networks

In our connected world, social media plays an important role in keeping people connected and informed. With Outlook being the hub of your calendar or schedule and contacts as well as your email, it makes sense to have Outlook also track and integrate your friends and colleagues through social media. If you and the people you want to exchange information with are on a social media site such as Facebook, LinkedIn, or Twitter, you can have updates from your friends appear in Outlook. Both you and your colleagues have to agree to share this information or have your updates publically available through the sites. The People Pane works as your hub for social media. Select an Outlook item such as an email or meeting request and click the sender or a recipient in that item. If you keep the People Pane open, you will be updated with activities, photos, and status updates of this person on the selected social networks. **CASE** *You explore the social media features of Outlook 2013 and apply them to your job in the human resources department.*

STEPS

1. **Click the People button in the Navigation Pane to view your contacts**

   See **FIGURE B-17**. Your screen will display different information, which is based on the people in your Contacts folder.

2. **Click the Connect to a social network link in the My Contacts pane, click Next to skip the information screen if a Microsoft Office dialog box opens**

   See **FIGURE B-18**. Currently, Facebook and LinkedIn are two popular sites; however, the social network sites listed in the Social Network Accounts dialog box may change over time. You can also connect to other networks by clicking More to find other social networks. If you select one of the networks by clicking its check box, you are prompted to log in to that social network using your username and password information for that social network.

3. **Click the Settings button**

   The Settings dialog box opens with three options for how you want the social network information to be updated in Outlook. You can be prompted before updating, you can have the updates appear in your Outlook without prompting, or you can never update the information.

4. **Click Cancel, click Finish, then click Yes if a message box opens**

   At this time, you will not set up the social connections.

5. **Click the HOME tab, then click People in the Current View group**

   When you do set up social connections, each generic icon in the contacts list and in the People Pane will be replaced with the profile picture that the contact has set in his or her social network profile.

6. **Click Mail in the Navigation Pane, click the VIEW tab, click the People Pane button in the People Pane group, click Normal to select it, then click All in the People Pane at the bottom of the Reading Pane**

   See **FIGURE B-19**. If you are connected, you will see updates for any person who sent or people who received the selected message.

FIGURE B-17: Viewing contact information as business cards

Business Card view

Link to connect to a social network

Contacts in Address Book (yours will differ)

Picture associated with this contact

FIGURE B-18: Setting up the social connector

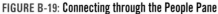

Click to select the social network site you want to connect to, then follow the on-screen directions to log in

Click to search for and then select a social network not listed

Click to open the Settings dialog box where you can change your settings regarding updates

FIGURE B-19: Connecting through the People Pane

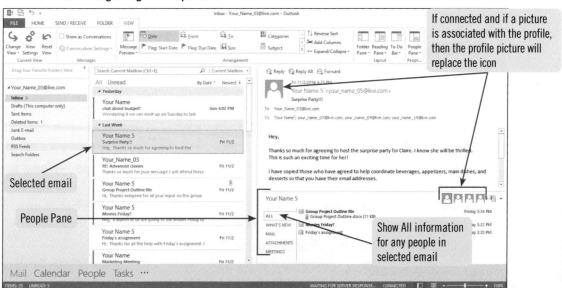

If connected and if a picture is associated with the profile, then the profile picture will replace the icon

Selected email

People Pane

Show All information for any people in selected email

Apply Categories

You use **categories** in Outlook to tag items so you can track and organize them by specific criteria. Outlook comes with color categories that are set by default. You can rename the colors as needed. For example, red can be urgent, blue can be business, and green can be personal. By assigning color categories to contacts, tasks, appointments, notes, or any item in Outlook, you can quickly filter and sort by color to review all items assigned to a specific color category. If you change your Contacts view to List view and then click the Categories button in the Arrangement section of the VIEW tab, you can see your contacts clearly by category. **CASE** ▶ *QST wants to use color to help organize information about its contacts and staff. Eventually, you will set up a system to assign colors to contacts and staff based on region.*

STEPS

1. **Click People in the Navigation Pane, then click Business Card in the Current View group**

2. **Click the Contact card for your name, then click the Categorize button in the Tags group on the HOME tab**

   Outlook comes with six predefined color categories: Blue , Green, Orange, Purple, Red, and Yellow.

3. **Click Green Category (or the name of the green category if its name has been changed)**

   Your Contact card is now assigned the color green.

4. **Double click the Contact card for your name**

   You can see the green color bar. You can also see the color categories assigned to contacts if you view your contacts as a list.

5. **Click the Close button ✕ to close your contact card, click People in the Navigation Pane, click the VIEW tab, click the Change View button in the Current view group, click the List button, then click the Categories button in the Arrangement group**

   The contacts are grouped by category, as shown in **FIGURE B-20**. Notice your contact information is listed with the other contacts in the green category.

6. **Click Calendar in the Navigation Pane, click the Week button in the Arrange group, click the Forward arrow to scroll to next week, click the Tuesday 10 AM time slot on the Calendar, type Benefits meeting, then press [Enter]**

   The Benefits meeting is entered in the calendar as an appointment and the CALENDAR TOOLS APPOINTMENT tab is active.

7. **Click the Categorize button in the Tags group, click Green Category (or the category's name), click the Categorize button in the Tags group, then click Purple Category (or the category's name)**

   The appointment is assigned the colors purple and green. If you view the calendar as a list and group by color category, the Benefits meeting will appear in both the purple and the green category groups.

8. **Click People in the Navigation Pane, click any Contact, click the HOME tab, click the Categorize button in the Tags group, then click All Categories to open the Color Categories dialog box, as shown in FIGURE B-21**

9. **Click Green Category (or the category's name), click Rename, type Personal as the new name, then click OK**

   The name of the green category changes to "Personal". To display the list of color categories and the name associated with each, click the HOME tab, then click the Categorize list arrow in the Tags group.

10. **Click the FILE tab, then click Exit to exit Outlook**

    As you work on other applications at your computer, you can leave Outlook open so you can refer to your contacts, be reminded of appointments, and see updates from any friends or colleagues connected through the social connector.

Managing Information Using Outlook

FIGURE B-20: Contacts grouped by color category

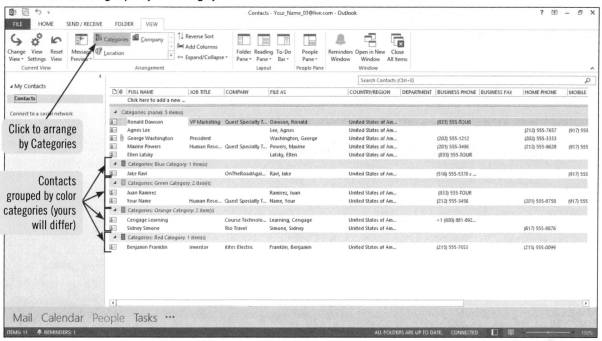

FIGURE B-21: Color Categories dialog box

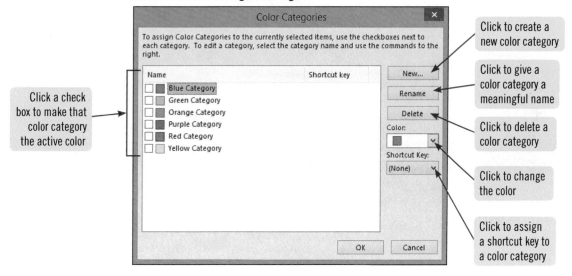

Coordinating calendars

Calendar can check the availability of all the people and resources for the meetings you want to set up. Once you select a meeting time and location, you can send invitations as meeting requests by entering contact names in the To text box, then clicking the Send button. The meeting request arrives in the invitee's Inbox with buttons to Accept, Reject, or Request a change directly in the email message. If an invitee accepts the invitation, a positive email reply is sent back to you, and Outlook posts the meeting to the invitee's calendar. If you share calendars through a network, you can click the Open Calendar button in the Manage Calendars group on the HOME tab, then click Open Shared Calendar to view the calendars of your colleagues. To send a copy of a time period in your calendar to someone through email, click the E-mail Calendar button in the Share group on the HOME tab, adjust the options in the Send a Calendar via Email dialog box, click OK, then address and send the email.

Practice

Concepts Review

Label each element of the Calendar window shown in FIGURE B-22.

FIGURE B-22

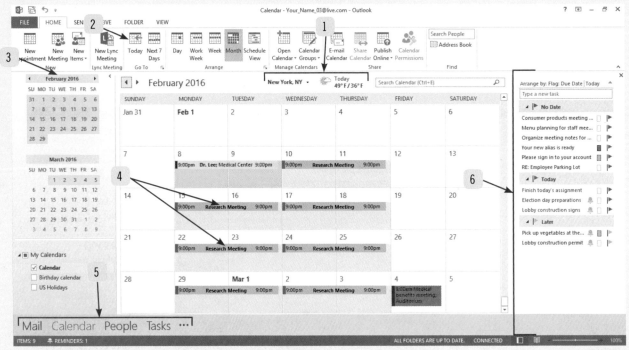

Match each term with the statement that best describes it.

7. Notes   **a.** Send and receive messages

8. Tasks   **b.** Keep and track appointments

9. Mail   **c.** Manage a to-do list

10. Calendar   **d.** Organize contacts

11. People   **e.** Jot down ideas or reminders

Select the best answer from the list of choices.

12. **Which of the following is *not* a module in Outlook?**
    - **a.** Mail
    - **b.** Calendar
    - **c.** Paint
    - **d.** Notes

13. **To color-code your appointments, meetings, contacts, and events, use:**
    - **a.** Flags.
    - **b.** Paint.
    - **c.** Categories.
    - **d.** Notes.

14. **If you want to be alerted when a task is due, you should set and use a:**
    - **a.** Category.
    - **b.** Reminder.
    - **c.** Flag.
    - **d.** Cluster.

15. **If Outlook can't identify an address component that you type in the Address text box, Outlook opens the_____ dialog box.**
    - **a.** Rules Wizard
    - **b.** Check Full Name
    - **c.** Check Address
    - **d.** Map It

16. **If you have a monthly meeting, create a(n): _____ .**
    - **a.** Recurring appointment.
    - **b.** Appointment reminder.
    - **c.** Event that lasts 24 hours or more.
    - **d.** Monthly event.

17. **If you enter a contact's birthday using the Details page, the date appears as a(n) _____ on the calendar.**
    - **a.** Email in the Inbox
    - **b.** Appointment for today
    - **c.** Repeating task
    - **d.** Recurring event

18. **If you want to quickly know the weather in your current city, use the_____ module.**
    - **a.** Mail
    - **b.** Calendar
    - **c.** People
    - **d.** Notes

19. **Which of these fields is only available when you click Details as you create a new Contact card?**
    - **a.** Web page
    - **b.** Company
    - **c.** Business address
    - **d.** Birthday

20. **When you enter an incomplete name that doesn't meet the field requirements in a new Contact card, Outlook:**
    - **a.** Closes the dialog box and cancels the contact.
    - **b.** Offers a list of possible suggestions.
    - **c.** Leaves the name as is.
    - **d.** Opens the Check Full Name dialog box.

Skills Review

1. **Describe Outlook.**
   - **a.** Start Outlook and view Mail.
   - **b.** Arrange the Outlook window so the Folder Pane is set to Normal, the Reading Pane is on the right, and the People Pane is set to Normal.
   - **c.** If there is any mail in the Inbox, click a message and view the message in the Reading Pane.
   - **d.** Click each tab on the Ribbon, and view the different command buttons.
   - **e.** Click Calendar, click People, click Tasks, then click Mail in the Navigation Pane.
   - **f.** Click the HOME tab on the Ribbon.

2. **Organize email.**
   - **a.** View the Inbox.
   - **b.** View the email in the Inbox by Date, with the most recent on top.
   - **c.** Select a message, review the People Pane, review the contents, then collapse the People Pane.

Skills Review (continued)

d. Open a New Message window, and write an email message to your instructor and at least one friend so there are two email addresses in the To box. Include an address in the Cc box, then type **Community Service Project** as the subject of the message. As the body of the message, enter the message shown in **FIGURE B-23**.

e. Send the message.

f. Open the Sent Items folder, review the emails, then return to the Inbox.

FIGURE B-23

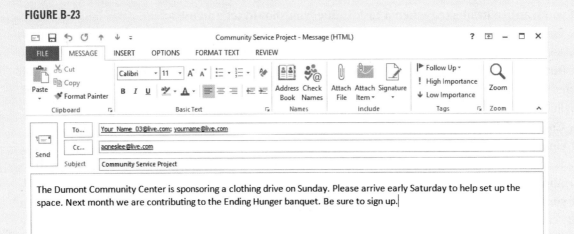

3. Manage your contacts.

a. Click People and view the Contacts.

b. Open a new untitled Contact window.

c. Create a new contact using the information in **FIGURE B-24**.

d. If you have a photo or any picture, add it to the Contact card.

e. Click the Details button in the Show group, enter January 17th as the birthday, then click Yes if a message dialog box opens.

f. Save and close the contact.

FIGURE B-24

Full Name...	Benjamin Franklin		**Benjamin Franklin**
Company	Kites Electric		Kites Electric
Job title	Inventor		Inventor
File as	Franklin, Benjamin		(215) 555-7653 Work

Internet

E-mail...	benfranklin@benfranklin.com
Display as	Benjamin Franklin (benfranklin@benfranklin.com)
Web page address	http://www2.fi.edu/
IM address	

Phone numbers

Business...	(215) 555-7653
Home...	(215) 555-0099
Business Fax...	
Mobile...	

Addresses

| Business... | 320 Market Street Philadelphia, PA 19101 |
| ✓ This is the mailing address | Map It |

Skills Review (continued)

4. Manage your calendar.

  a. Open the Calendar module.

  b. View the calendar by Week.

  c. Go to today.

  d. Scroll to January and view Ben Franklin's birthday.

  e. Return to today, create a new appointment for next week for a 2 1/2- hour lunch meeting with **Jennifer, Emily, and Michael** at noon at **Café Angelique**. Set a reminder for **1 day**. This appointment should be labeled **Out of Office**. (*Hint*: click the Show As list arrow, then click Out of Office.) Refer to **FIGURE B-25**.

  f. Save and close the appointment.

FIGURE B-25

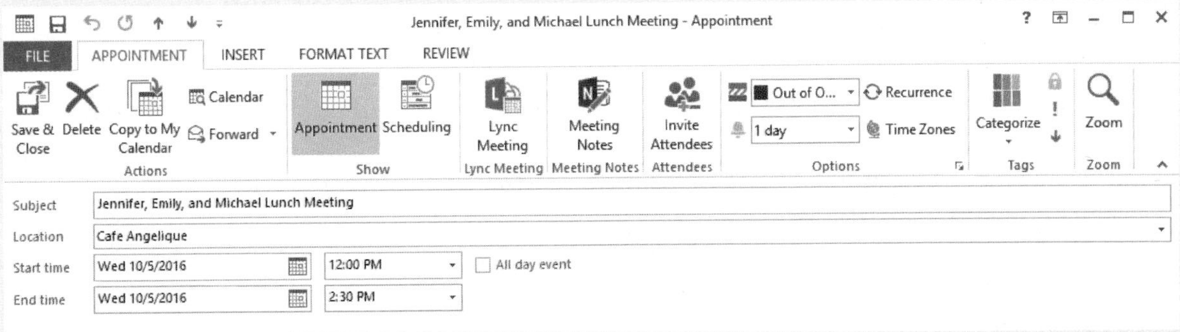

5. Manage tasks.

  a. Open Tasks.

  b. Create a new task with the subject of the task **Pick up vegetables at the CSA**.

  c. Start the new task next month.

  d. Set the reminder for 8 a.m. of the date you have to pick up the vegetables.

  e. Set this task as a high priority task. See **FIGURE B-26**.

  f. Save and close the task.

  g. View the task list in Simple List and Detailed List views.

FIGURE B-26

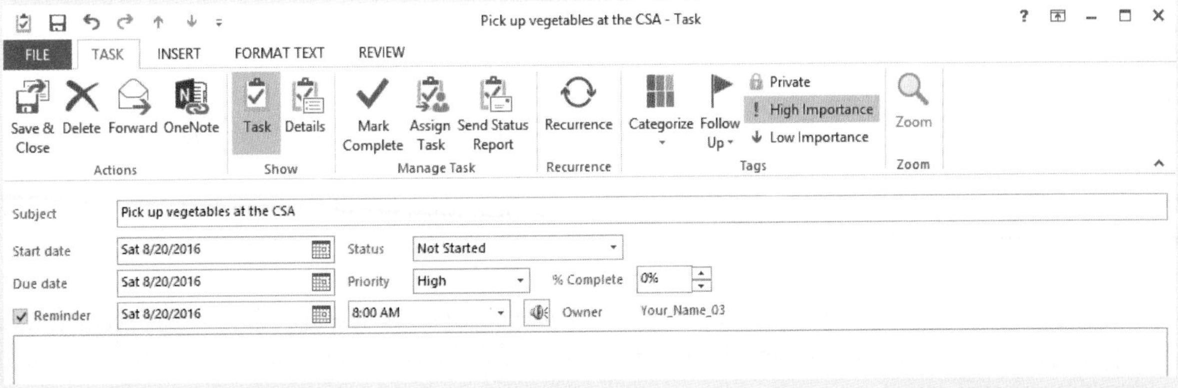

Skills Review (continued)

6. Create notes.

   a. Open Notes.

   b. Create a new note with the following text: **Post fliers in town hall about the new library hours.** See FIGURE B-27.

   c. Close the note.

7. Integrate social connectors.

   a. Click Mail in the Navigation Pane, open the People Pane, and then select any message in the Inbox.

   b. Click ALL in the People Pane, and view all information related to the person who sent the selected email.

   c. Click People in the Navigation Pane, click People in the Current View group, then review the contacts.

   d. Click the VIEW tab, click the People Pane button in the People Pane group, then click Account Settings.

   e. Click More to open a Web page about connecting to your favorite social network, then read the Web page that appears.

   f. Scroll down, click the Frequently asked questions link, then read the web page. (If you are not connected to the Internet, continue to the next step.)

   g. Click the Outlook button on the taskbar to return to Outlook, close the open dialog box, then view the contacts as business cards.

8. Apply categories.

   a. Open Contacts, then assign any color category to your Contact card.

   b. Assign a category to the lunch appointment that you created in Step 4.

   c. Assign a second category to the task you created in Step 5.

   d. View Contacts as a list grouped by category.

   e. View the Tasks as a list grouped by category.

   f. Exit Outlook.

FIGURE B-27

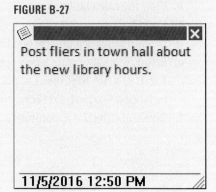

Independent Challenge 1

As manager of a local organic food co-op, your job is to develop contacts for all customers that come into the store and set the schedule for the volunteers. The contacts will also be used to send direct mail for future promotions. You created a form for customers to complete so you can gather their contact information. The information includes first and last name, mailing address, email address, and at least one phone number. Each week, you select one customer from the list of new names to receive a small prize package. You need to create the contacts in Outlook and use Outlook to schedule the weekly prize giveaway.

   a. Open Contacts in Outlook, and then create five new Contact cards. Use your friends' information or make up fictitious names and contact information.

   b. Create two notes, each in the Blue category, that remind you about two different events that take place in the store.

   c. Create a recurring appointment on each Thursday for the next 2 months to select a winner from the list of new names.

   d. Enter two new tasks in the task list. One task is for you to review the farmers markets in the area and contact them to participate in your store's events, and the other task is for you to review the local ordinances in town. Each task should have a start date of next week, a high priority, and be in the Yellow category.

   e. View the Calendar with the To-Do Bar open.

   f. Exit Outlook.

Independent Challenge 2: Explore

Outlook is an integrated information management system that stores information in folders specific to the type of information stored. You can create new folders for specific types of information and view them in the folders list. You can also transfer one type of item to another. For example, you can drag a task to the Calendar to create an appointment. The integration of the different types of information is what makes Outlook so powerful. You are going to move items from one Outlook module to another to see how easily you can integrate information. New tasks and messages will be created as you go through this exercise; save and close each one before moving to the next step.

a. Open Mail in Outlook, then drag an email message from the Inbox to Tasks in the Navigation Pane to create a new task. In a note in Outlook, explain what happens. What elements of the email message are entered in which task fields?

b. Drag an email message from the Inbox to Calendar in the Navigation Pane, then explain what happens.

c. Create a new Note, then drag the note to Calendar in the Navigation Pane, then explain what happens.

d. Open the Calendar, drag an existing appointment from the Calendar to Tasks in the Navigation Pane, then explain what happens.

e. Drag the same appointment you dragged in Step d to Mail in the Navigation Pane, then explain what happens.

f. Find the location for the Weather in the Calendar. Select another part of the country for the location. Did you notice a change in the weather information that is displayed? (If you are using a computer that is not connected to the Internet, skip this step.)

g. View the Contacts list in two different views.

h. Drag a Contact card from the Contacts list to Calendar in the Navigation Pane, then explain what happens.

i. Open an existing contact, click the Categorize button, then click All Categories.

j. Rename the Purple and Red categories to names of your choice, close the Color Categories dialog box, then assign the contact to both categories.

k. Save and close the contact.

l. Drag a Contact card from the Contacts list to Mail in the Navigation Pane, then explain what happens.

m. Create a new contact for yourself using the name of a favorite movie star and your personal information, add two categories, then send an email to yourself.

n. Open the Contact card for your name. Click the Map It button, print the screen that appears in a Web browser. (If you are using a computer that is not connected to the Internet, skip this step.)

o. Find a photo of yourself, and add it to your new contact card.

p. Print your contact card as directed by your instructor.

q. Exit Outlook.

Visual Workshop

Start Outlook. First, create a new contact, as shown in **FIGURE B-28**, using any photo you want. Create an appointment as shown in **FIGURE B-29**, using a weekday in the next 2 weeks as the date for the appointment. Finally, create a task, as shown in **FIGURE B-30**. Note that the dates in the figures will differ from those on your screen.

FIGURE B-28

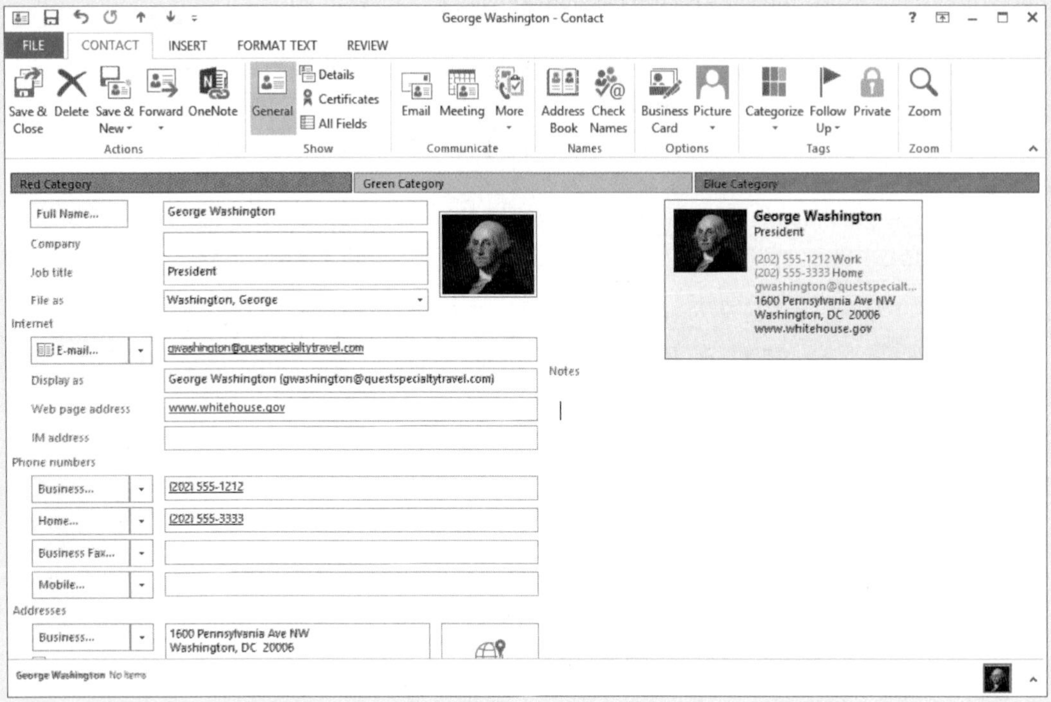

FIGURE B-29

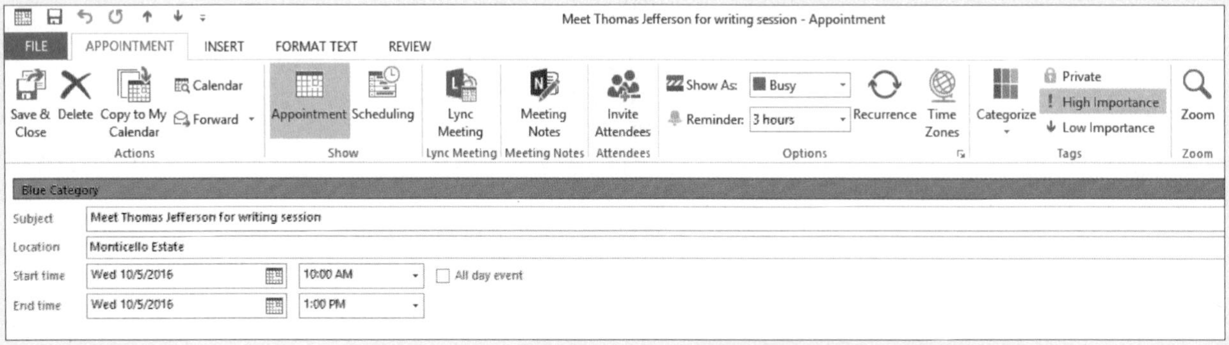

FIGURE B-30

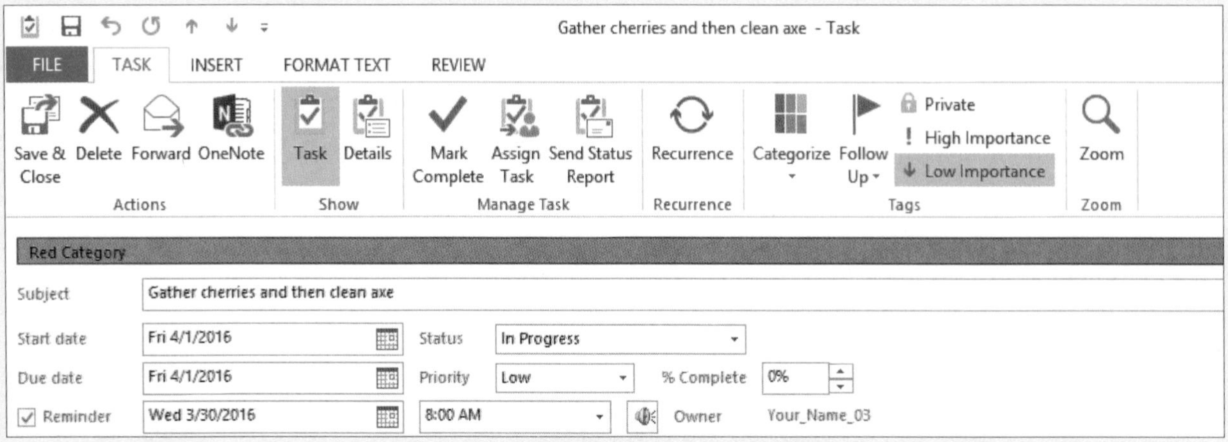

Working in the Cloud

CASE In your job for the Vancouver branch of Quest Specialty Travel, you travel frequently, you often work from home, and you also collaborate online with colleagues and clients. You want to learn how you can use SkyDrive with Office 2013 to work in the Cloud so that you can access and work on your files anytime and anywhere. (*Note*: SkyDrive and Office Web Apps are dynamic Web pages, and might change over time, including the way they are organized and how commands are performed. The steps and figures in this appendix reflect these pages at the time this book was published.)

Unit Objectives

After completing this unit, you will be able to:

- Understand Office 2013 in the Cloud
- Work Online
- Explore SkyDrive
- Manage Files on SkyDrive
- Share Files
- Explore Office Web Apps
- Complete a Team Project

Files You Will Need

WEB-1.pptx
WEB-2.docx

Understand Office 2013 in the Cloud

Learning
Outcomes
• Describe Office
2013 Cloud
Computing
features
• Define SkyDrive
• Define Office
Web Apps

The term **cloud computing** refers to the process of working with files and apps online. You may already be familiar with Web-based e-mail accounts such as Gmail and outlook.com. These applications are **cloud-based**, which means that you do not need a program installed on your computer to run them. Office 2013 has also been designed as a cloud-based application. When you work in Office 2013, you can choose to store your files "in the cloud" so that you can access them on any device connected to the Internet. **CASE** ▶ *You review the concepts related to working online with Office 2013.*

DETAILS

- ### How does Office 2013 work in the Cloud?

  When you launch an Office application such as Word or Excel, you might see your name and maybe even your picture in the top right corner of your screen. This information tells you that you have signed in to Office 2013, either with your personal account or with an account you are given as part of an organization such as a company or school. When you are signed in to Office and click the FILE tab in any Office 2013 application such as Word or Excel, you see a list of the files that you have used recently on your current computer and on any other connected device such as a laptop, a tablet or even a Windows phone. The file path appears beneath each filename so that you can quickly identify its location as shown in **FIGURE WEB-1**. Office 2013 also remembers your personalized settings so that they are available on all the devices you use.

- ### What are roaming settings?

  A **roaming setting** is a setting that travels with you on every connected device. Examples of roaming settings include your personal settings such as your name and picture, the files you've used most recently, your list of connected services such as Facebook and Twitter, and any custom dictionaries you've created. Two particularly useful roaming settings are the Word Resume Reading Position setting and the PowerPoint Last Viewed Slide setting. For example, when you open a PowerPoint presentation that you've worked on previously, you will see a message similar to the one shown in **FIGURE WEB-2**.

- ### What is SkyDrive?

  SkyDrive is an online storage and file sharing service. When you are signed in to your computer with your Microsoft account, you receive access to your own SkyDrive, which is your personal storage area on the Internet. On your SkyDrive, you are given space to store up to 7 GB of data online. A SkyDrive location is already created on your computer as shown in **FIGURE WEB-3**. Every file you save to SkyDrive is synced among your computers and your personal storage area on SkyDrive.com. The term **synced** (which stands for synchronized) means that when you add, change or delete files on one computer, the same files on your other devices are also updated.

- ### What are Office Web Apps?

  Office Web Apps are versions of Microsoft Word, Excel, PowerPoint, and OneNote that you can access online from your SkyDrive. An Office Web App does not include all of the features and functions included with the full Office version of its associated application. However, you can use the Office Web App from any computer that is connected to the Internet, even if Microsoft Office 2013 is not installed on that computer.

- ### How do SkyDrive and Office Web Apps work together?

  You can create a file in Office 2013 using Word, Excel, PowerPoint, or OneNote and then save it to your SkyDrive. You can then open the Office file saved to SkyDrive and edit it using your Office 2013 apps. If you do not have Office 2013 installed on the computer you are using, you can edit the file using your Web browser and the corresponding Office Web App. You can also use an Office Web App to create a new file, which is saved automatically to SkyDrive while you work and you can download a file created with an Office Web App and work with the file in the full version of the corresponding Office application.

FIGURE WEB-1: FILE tab in Microsoft Excel

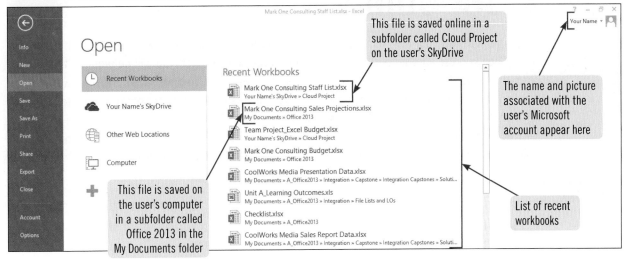

FIGURE WEB-2: PowerPoint Last Viewed Slide setting

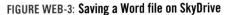

FIGURE WEB-3: Saving a Word file on SkyDrive

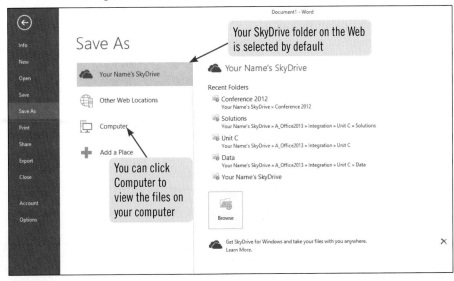

Work Online

Learning Outcomes
- View Microsoft account settings
- Sign out of a Microsoft account
- Switch Microsoft accounts

When you work on your own computer, you are usually signed in to your Microsoft account automatically. When you use another person's computer or a public computer, you will be required to enter the password associated with your Microsoft account to access files you have saved on Windows SkyDrive. You know you are signed in to Windows when you see your name and possibly your picture in the top right corner of your screen. *Note*: To complete the steps below, you need to be signed in to your Microsoft account. If you do not have a Microsoft account, see "Getting a Microsoft account" in the yellow box. **CASE** ▶ *You explore the settings associated with your account, learn how to switch accounts, and sign out of an account.*

STEPS

1. **Sign in to Windows, if necessary, launch Word, click** Blank document**, then verify that your name appears in the top right corner of your screen**

2. **Click the** list arrow **to the right of your name, as shown in** FIGURE WEB-4**, then click** About me **and sign in if prompted**

   Internet Explorer opens and your Profile page appears. Here, you can add or edit your contact information and information about your workplace. You can also change the name and picture that appear in the top right corner of your window.

3. **Click the** list arrow **next to Profile in the top left corner of your screen, above the picture**

   The tiles representing the services your Windows account is connected to appear as shown in **FIGURE WEB-5**. Note that if you have connected your Microsoft account to accounts in other services such as Facebook, LinkedIn, or outlook.com, you will see these connections in the appropriate app. For example, your connections to Facebook and LinkedIn appear in the People app.

4. **Click a blank area below the apps tiles, click** Your Name **in the top right corner, then click** Account settings

   Either you are taken directly to the Microsoft account screen or, depending on your security settings, a Sign in screen appears. To make changes to your account, you might need to enter the password associated with your account. You can also choose to sign in with a different Microsoft account. Once you sign in, you can change the information associated with your account such as your name, email address, birth date, and password. You can also choose to close your Microsoft account, which deletes all the data associated with it.

5. **Click the** Close button **⬛✕** **in the upper right corner of the window to remove the Sign-in window, click** Close all tabs **to return to Word, then click the** list arrow **▼** **next to Your Name in the top right corner of the Word window**

   To sign out of your account, you can click Sign Out at the top of the Accounts dialog box that appears when you click Account Settings. When you are working on your own computers, you will rarely need to sign out of your account. However, if you are working on a public computer, you may want to sign out of your account to avoid having your files accessible to other users.

6. **Click** Switch account

   You can choose to sign into another Microsoft account or to an account with an organization.

7. **Click the** Close button **✕**

   You are returned to a blank document in Word.

8. **Exit Word**

FIGURE WEB-4: Viewing Windows account options in Word

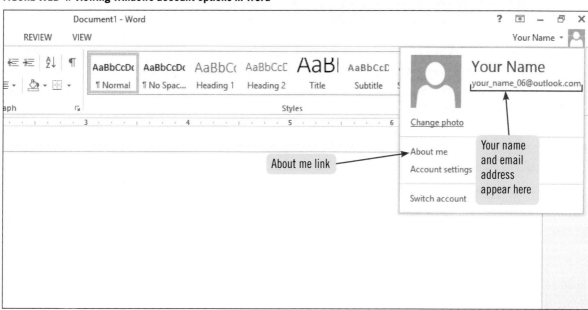

FIGURE WEB-5: Connected services associated with a Profile

Getting a Microsoft account

If you have been working with Windows and Office 2013, you might already have a Microsoft account, which was previously referred to as a Windows Live ID. You also have an account if you use outlook.com (formerly Hotmail), SkyDrive, Xbox LIVE, or have a Windows Phone. A Microsoft account consists of an email address and a password. If you wish to create a new Microsoft account, go to https://signup.live.com/ and follow the directions provided.

Explore SkyDrive

Learning Outcomes
• Save a file to SkyDrive
• Create a folder on SkyDrive

SkyDrive works like the hard drive on your computer. You can save and open files from SkyDrive, create folders, and manage your files. You can access the files you save on SkyDrive from any of your connected devices and from anywhere you have a computer connection. **CASE** ▶ *You open a PowerPoint presentation, save the file to your SkyDrive, then create a folder.*

STEPS

1. **Start PowerPoint, then open the file** WEB-1.pptx **from the location where you store your Data Files**

2. **Click the** FILE tab, **click** Save As, **then click** Your Name's SkyDrive **(top selection) if it is not already selected**

QUICK TIP
If you are signed in with your own account, you will see Your Name's Sky-Drive (for example, "Tom's SkyDrive").

3. **Click the** Browse button
   The Save As dialog box opens, showing the folders stored on your SkyDrive. You may have several folders already stored there or you may have none.

4. **Click** New folder, **type** Cengage, **then press** [Enter]

5. **Double-click** Cengage, **select** WEB-1.pptx **in the File name text box, type** WEB-QST Vancouver 1 **as shown in** FIGURE WEB-6, **then click** Save
   The file is saved to the Cengage folder on the SkyDrive that is associated with your Microsoft account. The PowerPoint window reappears.

6. **Click the** FILE tab, **click** Close, **click the** FILE tab, **then click** Open
   WEB-QST Vancouver 1.pptx appears as the first file listed in the Recent Presentations list, and the path to your Cengage folder on your SkyDrive appears beneath it.

7. **Click** WEB-QST Vancouver 1.pptx **to open it, then type your name where indicated on the title slide**

8. **Click** Slide 2 **in the Navigation pane, select** 20% **in the third bullet, type** 30%, **click the** FILE tab, **click** Save As, **click** Cengage **under Current Folder, change the file name to** WEB-QST Vancouver 2, **then click** Save

9. **Exit PowerPoint**
   A new version of the presentation is saved to the Cengage folder that you created on SkyDrive.

How to disable default saving to Skydrive

You can specify how you want to save files from Office 2013 applications. By default, files are saved to locations you specify on your SkyDrive. You can change the default to be a different location. In Word, PowerPoint, or Excel, click the FILE tab, then click Options. Click Save in the left sidebar, then in the Save section, click the Save to Computer by default check box, as shown in **FIGURE WEB-7**. Click OK to close the PowerPoint Options dialog box. The Save options you've selected will be active in Word, PowerPoint, and Excel, regardless of which application you were using when you changed the option.

FIGURE WEB-6: Saving a presentation to SkyDrive

FIGURE WEB-7: Changing the default Save location in PowerPoint

Manage Files on SkyDrive

You are automatically connected to SkyDrive when you sign into your Microsoft account and launch an Office 2013 application. You can also access SkyDrive through your Web browser or from the SkyDrive App in Windows 8. When you start the SkyDrive App, you can upload and download files, create folders, and delete files. You can also download the SkyDrive app to your tablet or other mobile device so you can access files wherever you have an Internet connection. When you access SkyDrive from Internet Explorer, you can do more file management tasks, including renaming and moving files. **CASE** *You explore how to work with SkyDrive from your Web browser and from the SkyDrive App.*

STEPS

1. **Launch Internet Explorer or another Web browser, type** skydrive.com **in the Address box, then press [Enter]**

   If you are signed in to your Microsoft account, your SkyDrive opens. If you are not signed in, the login page appears where you can enter the email address and password associated with your Microsoft account.

2. **Sign in if necessary, click the blue tile labeled** Cengage, **then right-click** WEB-QST Vancouver 1.pptx **as shown in** FIGURE WEB-8

   You can open the file in the PowerPoint Web App or in PowerPoint, download the file to your computer, share it, embed it, and perform other actions such as renaming and deleting.

3. **Click** Download, **click** Open **in the bar at the bottom of the screen, then click** Enable Editing

   The presentation opens in PowerPoint where you can save it to your computer hard drive or back to SkyDrive.

4. **Click the** DESIGN **tab, click the** More button ▼ **in the Themes group, select the** Wisp **theme, click the** FILE **tab, click** Save As, **click** Computer, **click** Browse, **navigate to a location on your computer or on an external drive such as a USB flash drive, click** Save, **then exit PowerPoint**

5. **Launch PowerPoint, then notice the files listed in the left pane under Recent**

   The file you just saved to your computer or external drive appears first and the file saved to the Cengage folder on SkyDrive appears second.

6. **Click the second listing, notice that the file is not updated with the Wisp design, then exit PowerPoint**

   When you download a file from SkyDrive, changes you make are not saved to the version on SkyDrive. You can also access SkyDrive from your Windows 8 screen by using the SkyDrive app.

7. **Show the Windows 8 Start screen, click the** SkyDrive tile, **open the Cengage folder, right-click** WEB-QST Vancouver 1, **view the buttons on the taskbar as shown in** FIGURE WEB-9, **click the** Delete button **on the taskbar, then click** Delete

8. **Right-click** WEB-QST Vancouver 2, **click the** New Folder button **on the taskbar, type** Illustrated, **then click** Create folder

   You can rename and move files in SkyDrive through Internet Explorer.

9. **Move the mouse pointer to the top of the screen until it becomes the hand pointer, drag to the bottom of the screen to close the SkyDrive App, click the** Internet Explorer **tile on the Start screen, go to** skydrive.com, **right-click** WEB-QST Vancouver 2 **on the SkyDrive site, click** Move to, **click the** ❯ **next to Cengage, click** Illustrated, **then click** Move

FIGURE WEB-8: **File management options on SkyDrive**

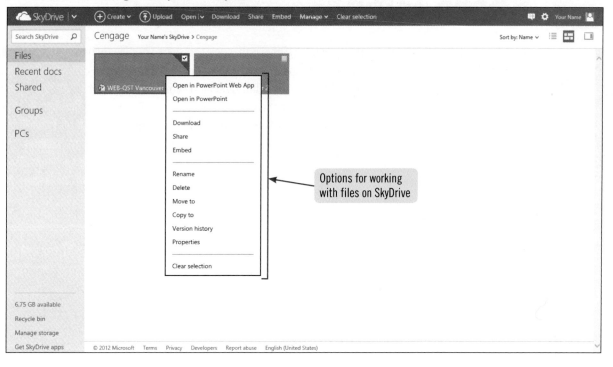

FIGURE WEB-9: **File management options on SkyDrive App**

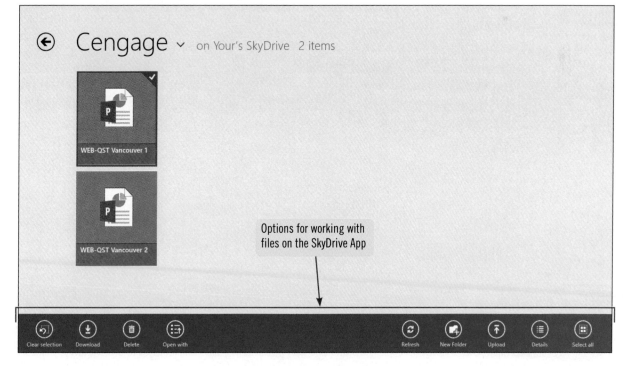

Share Files

One of the great advantages of working with SkyDrive is that you can share your files with others. Suppose, for example, that you want a colleague to review a presentation you created in PowerPoint and then add a new slide. You can, of course, e-mail the presentation directly to your colleague who can then make changes and e-mail the presentation back. Alternatively, you can share the PowerPoint file directly from SkyDrive. Your colleague can edit the file using the PowerPoint Web App or the full version of PowerPoint, and then you can check the updated file on SkyDrive. In this way, you and your colleague are working with just one version of the presentation that you both can update. **CASE** ▶ *You have decided to share files in the Illustrated folder that you created in the previous lesson with another individual. You start by sharing files with your partner and your partner can share files with you.*

STEPS

1. **Identify a partner with whom you can work, and obtain his or her e-mail address; you can choose someone in your class or someone on your e-mail list, but it should be someone who will be completing these steps when you are**

2. **Right-click the Illustrated folder, then click Sharing as shown in** FIGURE WEB-10

3. **Type the e-mail address of your partner**

4. **Click in the Include a personal message box, then type Here's the presentation we're working on together as shown in** FIGURE WEB-11

5. **Verify that the Recipients can edit check box is selected, then click Share**

   Your partner will receive a message advising him or her that you have shared the WEB-QST Vancouver 2.pptx file. If your partner is completing the steps at the same time, you will receive an e-mail from your partner.

6. **Check your e-mail for a message advising you that your partner has shared a folder with you**

   The subject of the e-mail message will be "[Name] has shared documents with you."

7. **If you have received the e-mail, click the Show content link that appears in the warning box, if necesary, then click WEB-QST Vancouver 2.pptx in the body of the e-mail message**

   The PowerPoint presentation opens in the Microsoft PowerPoint Web App. You will work in the Web App in the next lesson.

Co-authoring documents

You can work on a document, presentation, or workbook simultaneously with a partner. First, save the file to your SkyDrive. Click the FILE tab, click Share, then click Invite People. Enter the email addresses of the people you want to work on the file with you and then click Share. Once your partner has received, opened, and started editing the document, you can start working together. You will see a notification in the status bar that someone is editing the document with you. When you click the notification, you can see the name of the other user and their picture if they have one attached to their Windows account. When your partner saves, you'll see his or changes in green shading which goes away the next time you save. You'll have an opportunity to co-author documents when you complete the Team Project at the end of this appendix.

FIGURE WEB-10: Sharing a file from SkyDrive

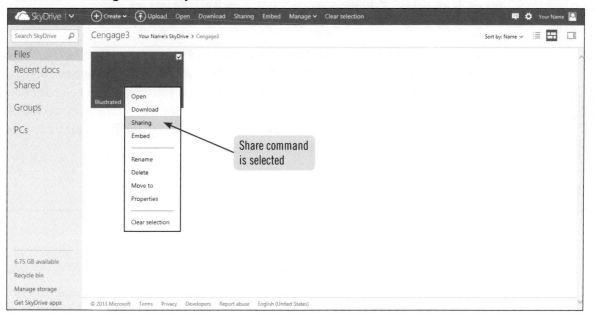

Share command
is selected

FIGURE WEB-11: Sharing a file with another person

Send email
Post to 🔵 🐦 💼
Get a link

Send a link to "WEB-QST Vancouver 2.pptx" in email

To

PartnerName@partneremail.com ✕

Here's the presentation we're working on together.

☑ Recipients can edit
☐ Require everyone who accesses this to sign in

Share   Cancel

Help me choose how to share

Explore Office Web Apps

As you have learned, a Web App is a scaled-down version of an Office program. Office Web Apps include Word, Excel, PowerPoint, and OneNote. You can use the Office Web Apps to create and edit documents even if you don't have Office 2013 installed on your computer and you can use them on other devices such as tablets and smartphones. From SkyDrive, you can also open the document in the full Office application if the application is installed on the computer you are using. **CASE** *You use the PowerPoint Web App and the full version of PowerPoint to edit the presentation.*

STEPS

1. **Click EDIT PRESENTATION, then click Edit in PowerPoint Web App**

   Presentations opened using the PowerPoint Web App have the same look and feel as presentations opened using the full version of PowerPoint. However, like all of the Office Web Apps, the PowerPoint Web App has fewer features available than the full version of PowerPoint.

2. **Review the Ribbon and its tabs to familiarize yourself with the commands you can access from the PowerPoint Web App**

   TABLE WEB-1 summarizes the commands that are available.

3. **Click Slide 3, click the text Hornby Island, click it again and select it, then type Tofino so the bullet item reads Tofino Sea Kayaking**

4. **Click outside the text box, click the DESIGN tab, then click the More Themes list arrow ▼ to show the selection of designs available**

   A limited number of designs are available on the PowerPoint Web App. When you want to use a design or a command that is not available on the PowerPoint Web App, you open the file in the full version of PowerPoint.

5. **Click on a blank area of the slide, click OPEN IN POWERPOINT at the top of the window, then click Yes in response to the message**

6. **Click the DESIGN tab, click the More button ▼ in the Themes group to expand the Themes gallery, select the Quotable design as shown in FIGURE WEB-12, click the picture on Slide 1, then press [Delete]**

7. **Click the Save button 🖫 on the Quick Access toolbar**

   The Save button includes a small icon indicating you are saving to SkyDrive and not to your computer's hard drive or an external drive.

8. **Click the Close button ✕ to exit PowerPoint**

   You open the document again to verify that your partner made the same changes.

9. **Launch PowerPoint, click WEB-QST Vancouver 2.pptx at the top of the Recent list, verify that the Quotable design is applied and the picture is removed, then exit PowerPoint**

Exploring other Office Web Apps

Three other Office Web Apps are Word, Excel, and OneNote. You can share files on SkyDrive directly from any of these applications using the same method you used to share files from PowerPoint. To familiarize yourself with the commands available in PowerPoint. To familiarize yourself with the commands available in an Office Web App, open the file and then review the commands on each tab on the Ribbon. If you want to perform a task that is not available in the Web App, open the file in the full version of the application.

FIGURE WEB-12: Selecting the Quotable design

TABLE WEB-1: Commands on the PowerPoint Web App

tab	category/group	options
FILE	Info	• Open in PowerPoint (also available on the toolbar above the document window)
		• Previous Versions
	Save As	• Where's the Save Button?: In PowerPoint Web App, the presentation is being saved automatically so there is no Save button
		• Download: use to download a copy of the presentation to your computer
	Print	• Create a printable PDF of the presentation that you can then open and print
	Share	• Share with people - you can invite others to view and edit your presentation
		• Embed - include the presentation in a blog on Web site
	About	• Try Microsoft Office, Terms of Use, and Privacy and Cookies
	Help	• Help with PowerPoint questions, Give Feedback to Microsoft, and modify how you can view the presentation (for example, text only)
	Exit	• Close the presentation and exit to view SkyDrive folders
HOME	Clipboard	• Cut, Copy, Paste, Format Painter
	Delete	• Delete a slide
	Slides	• Add a new slide, duplicate a slide, hide a slide
	Font	• Change the font, size, style, and color of selected text
	Paragraph	• Add bullets and numbering, indent text, align text, and change text direction
	Drawing	• Add text boxes and shapes, arrange them on the slide, apply Quick Styles, modify shape fill and outline, and duplicate a shape
INSERT	Slides	• Add new slides with selected layout
	Images	• Add pictures from your computer, online pictures, or screen shots
	Illustrations	• Add shapes, SmartArt, or charts
	Links	• Add links or actions to objects
	Text	• Add comments, text boxes, headers and footers, and other text elements
	Comments	• Add comments
DESIGN	Themes	• Apply a limited number of themes to a presentation and apply variants to a selected theme
		• Apply variants to a selected theme
ANIMATIONS	Animation	• Apply a limited number of animation effects to a slide element and modify existing timings
TRANSITIONS	Transitions to This Slide	• Apply a limited number of transition effects to slides and chose to apply the effect to all slides
VIEW	Presentation Views	• You can view the slide in Editing View, Reading View, Slide Show View, and Notes View and you can show any comments made by users who worked on PowerPoint using the full version

Team Project

Introduction

From SkyDrive, you can easily collaborate with others to produce documents, presentations, and spreadsheets that include each user's input. Instead of emailing a document to colleagues and then waiting for changes, you can both work on the document at the same time online. To further explore how you can work with SkyDrive and Office 2013, you will work with two other people to complete a team project. The subject of the team project is the planning of a special event of your choice, such as a class party, a lecture, or a concert. The special event should be limited to a single afternoon or evening.

Follow the guidelines provided below to create the files required for the team project. When you have completed the project, the team will submit a Word document containing information about your project, as well as three files related to the project: a Word document, a PowerPoint presentation, and an Excel workbook.

Project Setup

As a team, work together to complete the following tasks.

a. Share email addresses among all three team members.

b. Set up a time (either via email, an online chat session, Internet Messaging, or face to face) when you will get together to choose your topic and assign roles.

c. At your meeting, complete the table below with information about your team and your special event.

Team Name (last name of one team member or another name that describes the project.)
Team Members
Event type (for example, party, lecture, concert, etc.)
Event purpose (for example, fundraiser for a specific cause, celebrate the end of term, feature a special guest, etc.)
Event location, date, and time
Team Roles indicate who is responsible for each of the following three files (one file per team member)
Word document:
Excel workbook:
PowerPoint presentation:

Document Development

Individually, complete the tasks listed below for the file you are responsible for. You need to develop appropriate content, format the file attractively, and then be prepared to share the file with the other team members.

Word Document

The Word document contains a description of your special event and includes a table listing responsibilities and a time line. Create the Word document as follows:

1. Create a Cloud Project folder on your SkyDrive, then create a new Word document and save it as **Cloud Project_ Word Description** to the Cloud Project folder.

Document Development (continued)

2. Include a title with the name of your project and a subtitle with the names of your team members. Format the title with the Title style and the subtitle with the Subtitle style.

3. Write a paragraph describing the special event—its topics, purpose, the people involved, etc. You can paraphrase some of the information your team discussed in your meeting.

4. Create a table similar to the table shown below and then complete it with the required information. Include up to ten rows. A task could be "Contact the caterers" or "Pick up the speaker." Visualize the sequence of tasks required to put on the event.

Task	Person Responsible	Deadline

5. Format the table using the table style of your choice.

6. Save the document to your SkyDrive. You will share the document with your team members and receive feedback in the next section.

Excel Workbook

The Excel workbook contains a budget for the special event. Create the Excel workbook as follows:

1. Create a new Excel workbook and save it as **Cloud Project_Excel Budget** to the Cloud Project folder on your SkyDrive.

2. Create a budget that includes both the revenues you expect from the event (for example, ticket sales, donations, etc.) and the expenses. Expense items include advertising costs (posters, ads, etc.), food costs if the event is catered, transportation costs, etc. The revenues and expenses you choose will depend upon the nature of the project.

3. Make the required calculations to total all the revenue items and all the expense items.

4. Calculate the net profit (or loss) as the revenue minus the expenses.

5. Format the budget attractively using fill colors, border lines, and other enhancements to make the data easy to read.

6. Save the workbook to your SkyDrive. You will share the workbook with your team members and receive feedback in the next section.

PowerPoint Presentation

The PowerPoint presentation contains a presentation that describes the special event to an audience who may be interested in attending. Create the PowerPoint presentation as follows:

1. Create a new PowerPoint presentation and save it as **Cloud Project_PowerPoint Presentation** to the Cloud Project folder on your SkyDrive.

2. Create a presentation that consists of five slides including the title slide as follows:
   a. Slide 1: Title slide includes the name of the event and your team members
   b. Slide 2: Purpose of the party or event
   c. Slide 3: Location, time, and cost
   d. Slide 4: Chart showing a breakdown of costs (to be supplied when you co-author in the next section)
   e. Slide 5: Motivational closing slide designed to encourage the audience to attend; include appropriate pictures

3. Format the presentation attractively using the theme of your choice.

4. Save the presentation to your SkyDrive. You will share the presentation with your team members and receive feedback.

Co-Authoring on Skydrive

You need to share your file, add feedback to the other two files, then create a final version of your file. When you read the file created by the other two team members, you need to add additional data or suggestions. For example, if you created the Excel budget, you can provide the person who created the PowerPoint presentation with information about the cost breakdown. If you created the Word document, you can add information about the total revenue and expenses contained in the Excel budget to your description. You decide what information to add to each of the two files you work with.

1. Open the file you created.
2. Click the **FILE tab**, click **Share**, then click **Invite People**.
3. Enter the email addresses of the other two team members, then enter the following message: **Here's the file I created for our team project. Please make any changes, provide suggestions, and then save it. Thanks!** See FIGURE WEB-13.

FIGURE WEB-13

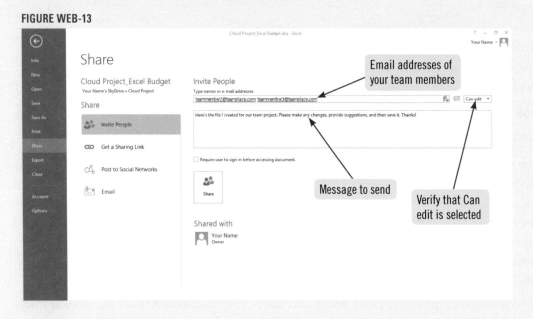

4. Click the **Share button**.
5. Allow team members time to add information and comments to your file. Team members should save frequently. When the file is saved, it is saved directly to your SkyDrive. Note that you can work together on the document or you can work separately. You can also choose to make changes with the full version of the Office 2013 applications or with the Office Web Apps. When someone is working on your file, you will see their user name on the status bar.
6. Decide which changes you want to keep, make any further changes you think are needed to make the document as clear as possible, then save a final version.

Project Summary

When you are pleased with the contents of your file and have provided feedback to your team members, assign a team member to complete the following tasks and then complete your portion as required.

1. Open **WEB-2.docx** from the location where you save your Data Files, then save it to your Cloud Project folder on your SkyDrive as **Cloud Project_Summary**.
2. Read the directions in the document, then enter your name as Team Member 1 and write a short description of your experience working with SkyDrive and Office 2013 to complete the team project.
3. Share the file with your team members and request that they add their own names and descriptions.
4. When all team members have finished working on the document, save all the changes.
5. Make sure you store all four files completed for the project in the Cloud Project appendix on your SkyDrive, then submit them to your instructor on behalf of your team.

Glossary

Account Log-on information including ISP, email address, and password for each person using Outlook; used to create folders in Outlook for contacts, email, and schedules. *See also* Personal account.

Active The currently available document, program, or object; on the taskbar, when more than one program is open, the button for the active program appears slightly lighter.

Address book A stored list of names and email addresses that you can access through an email program such as Outlook to address messages.

Appointment In the Outlook Calendar module, an activity that does not involve inviting other people or scheduling resources.

Attachment A file, such as a picture, audio clip, video clip, document, worksheet, or presentation, that is sent in addition to the email message composed by typing in the message window.

Backstage view Appears when then FILE tab is clicked. The navigation bar on the left side contains commands to perform actions common to most Office programs, such as opening a file, saving a file, and closing the file.

Backward-compatible Software feature that enables documents saved in an older version of a program to be opened in a newer version of the program.

Blind courtesy copy (BCC) In email, a way to send a message to a recipient who needs to be aware of the correspondence between the sender and the recipients but who is not the primary recipient of the message and whose address is not visible to other recipients of the email; used when the sender does not want to reveal who has received courtesy copies.

Calendar module In Outlook, the module that provides a convenient way to manage appointments and events.

Categories In Outlook, a feature used to tag items so you can track and organize them by specific criteria.

Clipboard A temporary Windows storage area that holds the selections you copy or cut.

Cloud-based Apps that run in the cloud rather than via a program installed on your computer.

Cloud computing Work done in a virtual environment using data, applications, and resources stored on servers and accessed over the Internet or a company's internal network rather than on users' computers.

Compatibility The ability of different programs to work together and exchange data.

Computer network The hardware and software that make it possible for two or more computers to share information and resources.

Contacts In Outlook, all information related to people, such as business associates and personal friends.

Contact Group A named subset of the people in your Outlook Contacts folder, the named group includes the email addresses for all people in the group so you can send a message or invitation to everyone in the group at once. *See also* Distribution list.

Contextual tab A tab that displays only when a specific task can be performed: they appear in an accent color and close when no longer needed.

Conversations Emails that discuss a common subject or thread.

Courtesy copy (CC) In email, a way to send a message to a recipient who needs to be aware of the correspondence between the sender and the recipients but who is not the primary recipient of the message.

Date Navigator A monthly calendar in the To-Do Bar that gives you an overview of the month.

Deleted Items The folder that stores items when you delete or erase a message from any email folder, which means a deleted item, such as an email or contact card, is actually stored rather than being immediately and permanently deleted. *Also called* Trash folder.

Dialog box launcher An icon you can click to open a dialog box or task pane from which to choose related commands.

Distribution list A collection of contacts to whom you want to send the same messages; makes it possible for you to send a message to the same group without having to select each contact in the group. *See also* Contact Group.

Document window Most of the screen in any given program, where you create a document, slide, or worksheet.

Drafts The folder that stores unfinished messages that you can finish writing at a later time; many email programs automatically save unsent messages at regular intervals in the Drafts folder as a safety measure.

Electronic mail (email) The technology that makes it possible for you to send and receive messages through the Internet.

Email message A message sent using email technology.

Email software A computer program that enables you to send and receive email messages over a network, within an intranet, and through the Internet.

Emoticon A symbol created by combining keyboard characters; used to communicate feelings in emails.

Event In the Outlook Calendar module, an activity that lasts 24 hours or longer.

Field In an Outlook contact, an area that stores one piece of information, such as a first name or an email address.

File An electronic collection of stored data that has a unique name, distinguishing it from other files.

Filter Used to search for only specific information; for example, in Outlook Contacts, you can filter to view only those contacts who live in New Jersey.

Flag A method of coding email messages by assigning different colored flags to the messages to categorize them or indicate their level of importance for follow up.

Forwarding Sending an email message you have received to someone else.

Gallery A visual collection of choices you can browse through to make a selection. Often available with Live Preview.

Groups Each tab on the Ribbon is arranged into groups to make features easy to find.

Inbox An email folder that stores all incoming email.

Insertion point A blinking vertical line that appears when you click in the formula bar or in an active cell; indicates where new text will be inserted.

Integrate To incorporate a document and parts of a document created in one program into another program; for example, to incorporate an Excel chart into a PowerPoint slide, or an Access table into a Word document.

Interface The look and feel of a program; for example, the appearance of commands and the way they are organized in the program window.

Junk email Unwanted email that arrives from unsolicited sources. *Also called* spam. Also a default folder in Outlook for junk email.

Label In some email programs, the ability to assign an indicator to an email message to help sort or organize your email messages.

Launch To open or start a program on your computer.

Live Preview A feature that lets you point to a choice in a gallery or palette and see the results in the document without actually clicking the choice.

MapIt An Outlook feature on a Contact card that lets you view a contact's address on a map.

Mail module In Outlook, lets you manage all email.

Meeting In the Outlook Calendar module, an activity you invite people to or reserve resources for.

Message body In an email message, where you write the text of your message.

Message header Contains the basic information about a message including the sender's name and email address, the names and email addresses of recipients and CC recipients, a date and time stamp, and the subject of the message.

Message threading Message threading allows you to navigate through a group of messages, seeing all replies and forwards from all recipients; includes all emails that discuss a common subject.

Navigation Pane Typically on the left side of the Outlook window in Normal view; shows you the folder list in addition to the navigation shortcuts to select an Outlook module.

Notes module In Outlook, the electronic version of the sticky notes you buy at your local stationery store; a convenient way to quickly jot down a reminder or an idea.

Office Web Apps Versions of the Microsoft Office applications with limited functionality that are available online from SkyDrive. Users can view documents online and then edit them in the browser using a selection of functions.

Online collaboration The ability to incorporate feedback or share information across the Internet or a company network or intranet.

Outbox A temporary storage folder for email messages that have not yet been sent.

Outlook Today A feature in Outlook that shows your day at a glance, like an electronic version of a daily planner book; when it is open, you can see what is happening in the Calendar, Tasks, and Messages for the day.

Peek A feature in Outlook that opens a small window when you mouse over an event, task, or some activity and shows you a snapshot of the details for the item.

People module In Outlook, the module where you manage all your business and personal contact information.

People Pane Available in several Outlook views; shows you any social media information available for the person sending the current message and included files, appointments, and notes related to that person.

Personal account In Outlook, identifies you as a user with information such as your email address and password, the type of Internet service provider (ISP) you are using, and the incoming and outgoing email server address for your ISP. *See also* account.

Previewing Prior to printing, seeing onscreen exactly how the printed document will look.

Quick **Access toolbar** A small toolbar on the left side of a Microsoft application program window's title bar, containing icons that you click to quickly perform common actions, such as saving a file.

Really **Simple Syndication (RSS)** A format for feeding or syndicating news or any content from Web sites to your computer.

Ribbon Appears beneath the title bar in every Office program window, and displays commands you're likely to need for the current task.

Roaming setting A setting that travels with you on every connected device.

Rule In Outlook, enables you to organize your email by setting parameters for incoming email; for example, you can specify that all email from a certain person goes into the folder for a specific project.

Screen **capture** An electronic snapshot of your screen, as if you took a picture of it with a camera, which you can paste into a document.

Sent Items When you send an email message, a copy of the message is stored in this folder to help you track the messages you send out.

Service provider The organization or company that provides email or Internet access. *See also* Internet Service Provider.

SkyDrive An online storage and file sharing service.

Sort To reorder email message information, such as by date.

Spam Unwanted email that arrives from unsolicited sources. *Also called* junk email.

Spamming The sending of identical or near-identical unsolicited messages to a large number of recipients. Many email programs have filters that identify this email and place it in a special folder.

Subject line Meaningful text in the subject text box of an email message providing recipients with an idea of the message content.

Suite A group of programs that are bundled together and share a similar interface, making it easy to transfer skills and program content among them.

Synced The process by which files on your other devices are updated when you add, change, or delete files on one computer.

Tabs Organizational unit used for commands on the Ribbon. The tab names appear at the top of the Ribbon and the active tab appears in front.

Task In Outlook, an item in the Tasks module.

Tasks module In Outlook, the electronic to-do list, whereby each task has a subject, a start and end date, priority, and a description.

Theme A predefined set of colors, fonts, line and fill effects, and other formats that can be applied to an Excel worksheet and give it a consistent, professional look.

Title bar Appears at the top of every Office program window; displays the document name and program name.

Trash folder *See* Deleted Items folder.

User **interface** A collective term for all the ways you interact with a software program.

Username The first part of an email address that identifies the person who receives the email that is sent to this email address.

Vacation response An automatically-generated email message you can have sent in response to received emails when you are away; most email programs allow you to create a vacation response.

Views Display settings that show or hide selected elements of a document or module in the program window to make it easier to focus on a certain task, such as formatting or reading text.

View A method of displaying a document window to show more or fewer details or a different combination of elements that makes it easier to complete certain tasks, such as formatting or reading text.

Web-based email Web site that provides free email addresses and service.

Zooming in A feature that makes a document appear larger but shows less of it on screen at once; does not affect actual document size.

Zooming out A feature that shows more of a document on screen at once but at a reduced size; does not affect actual document size.

Index

SPECIAL CHARACTERS
@ (at sign), OUT 4, OUT 5

A

About command, PowerPoint Web App, CL 13
Access, OFF 2, OFF 3. *See also* field(s)
  filename and file extension, OFF 8
account(s)
  Microsoft. *See* Microsoft account
  personal, OUT 26
address book(s), OUT 4
Address book button, OUT 12
Animation command, PowerPoint Web App, CL 13
ANIMATIONS tab
  PowerPoint Web App, CL 13
app(s)
  launching, OFF 4–5
  starting, OFF 4, OFF 5
application(s)
  cloud-based, CL 2
  Office Web Apps. *See* Office Web Apps
appointment(s), OUT 32, OUT 33
Appointment Recurrence dialog box, OUT 32, OUT 33
at sign (@)
  email addresses, OUT 4, OUT 5
Attach File button, OUT 14
attachment(s), email, OUT 14–15
automatic responses, email, OUT 11

B

Backstage view, OFF 6, OFF 7
backward compatibility, OFF 11
Block Senders List, OUT 28
business cards, electronic, OUT 33

C

Calendar module, OUT 27, OUT 32–33
CALENDAR TOOLS APPOINTMENT tab, Categorize button, OUT 40
categories, OUT 40–41
Categorize button
  CALENDAR TOOLS APPOINTMENT tab, OUT 40
  HOME tab, OUT 40
Cc text box, OUT 6
Check Full Name dialog box, OUT 30
Clean Up tools, OUT 16, OUT 17
clipboard. *See* Office Clipboard; system clipboard

Clipboard command, PowerPoint Web App, CL 13
cloud computing, OFF 9
  definition, CL 2
  SkyDrive. *See* SkyDrive
cloud-based applications, CL 2
  Office Web Apps. *See* Office Web Apps
color categories, OUT 40, OUT 41
Color Categories dialog box, OUT 40, OUT 41
color-coding email messages, OUT 13
Comments command, PowerPoint Web App, CL 13
compatibility, OFF 2
Compatibility Mode, OFF 11
COMPOSE TOOLS MESSAGE tab, OUT 10, OUT 11
computer networks, OUT 2
contact(s)
  address books, OUT 4
  coordinating calendars, OUT 41
  managing, OUT 30–31
contact lists, email, OUT 17
conversations, showing email messages as, OUT 28
coordinating calendars, OUT 41
copying
  items using Office Clipboard, OFF 5
  notes, OUT 36
Customize Outlook Today pane, OUT 37
Customize Quick Access Toolbar button, OFF 12
customizing
  Outlook Today, OUT 37
cutting items, Office Clipboard, OFF 5

D

Date Navigator, OUT 26, OUT 32
Delete command, PowerPoint Web App, CL 13
Deleted Items folder, OUT 8, OUT 9
deleting
  email messages, OUT 16, OUT 17
delivery confirmation messages, OUT 2
DESIGN tab
  PowerPoint Web App, CL 13
desktop
  saving files to, OFF 8
dialog box launcher, OFF 6, OFF 7
distribution lists, email, OUT 17
document(s), OFF 12. *See also* file(s)
  co-authoring, CL 10
Document Recovery task pane, OFF 15
document window, OFF 6, OFF 7
Drafts folder, OUT 8, OUT 9
dragging
  notes, OUT 36

Drawing command, PowerPoint Web App, CL 13
duplicating. *See* copying

E

electronic business cards, OUT 33
electronic mail. *See* email
email
    attachments, OUT 14–15
    automatic responses, OUT 11
    color-coding messages, OUT 13
    contact lists, OUT 17
    creating messages, OUT 6, OUT 7
    deleting messages, OUT 16, OUT 17
    delivery confirmation messages, OUT 2
    distribution lists, OUT 17
    filtering, OUT 28
    flagging messages, OUT 13, OUT 34
    folders, OUT 8–9
    forwarding, OUT 12–13, OUT 16
    good practices, OUT 16–17
    junk (spam), OUT 8
    labeling messages, OUT 13
    managing, OUT 9
    message body, OUT 6, OUT 7
    message header, OUT 6, OUT 7
    organizing, OUT 2, OUT 28–29
    overview, OUT 2–3
    precautions regarding messages, OUT 12
    previewing messages, OUT 10
    receiving, OUT 10, OUT 11
    replying to messages, OUT 10, OUT 11
    rules, OUT 28, OUT 29
    sending messages, OUT 6, OUT 7
    shortcuts, OUT 16
    showing as conversations, OUT 28
    sorting, OUT 28–29
    subject line, OUT 6, OUT 7
    vacation responses, OUT 11
email addresses, OUT 4–5
email service providers, OUT 4, OUT 5
email software, OUT 2
emoticons, OUT 16
Empty Folder button, OUT 8
events, OUT 32
Excel, OFF 2, OFF 3
    filename and file extension, OFF 8
    Office Web App, CL 12
Exit command, PowerPoint Web App, CL 13

F

field(s)
    People module, OUT 30
file(s), OFF 10, OFF 11. *See also* document(s)
    attaching to email messages, OUT 14–15
    blank, creating, OFF 8
    creating, OFF 8, OFF 9
    definition, OFF 8
    integrating, OFF 2

    names, OFF 8
    opening, OFF 10, OFF 11
    recovering, OFF 15
    saving. *See* saving files; saving files to Skydrive
    sharing, SkyDrive, CL 10–11
file extensions, OFF 8
file management, SkyDrive, CL 8–9
FILE tab, CL 2, CL 3, OFF 7
    PowerPoint Web App, CL 13
filtering
    email messages, OUT 28
flagging email messages, OUT 13, OUT 34
folder(s)
    email, OUT 8–9
Folder Pane, OUT 32
FOLDER tab
    Empty Folder button, OUT 8
    managing folders, OUT 8
    New Folder button, OUT 9
Font command, PowerPoint Web App, CL 13
Forward button, OUT 12
forwarding emails, OUT 12–13, OUT 16

G

Gmail, labeling email messages, OUT 13
group(s), OFF 6

H

Help button, OFF 14
Help command, PowerPoint Web App, CL 13
Help window, OFF 14, OFF 15
HOME tab
    Categorize button, OUT 40
    Forward button, OUT 12
    New Email button, OUT 10, OUT 14
    New Note button, OUT 36, OUT 37
    PowerPoint Web App, CL 13

I

Illustrations command, PowerPoint Web App, CL 13
Images command, PowerPoint Web App, CL 13
Inbox folder, OUT 8, OUT 9
Info command, PowerPoint Web App, CL 13
Insert File dialog box, OUT 14, OUT 15
INSERT tab
    PowerPoint Web App, CL 13
insertion point, OFF 8
integrating
    files, OFF 2
interface, OFF 2

J

Junk E-mail folder, OUT 8, OUT 9

L

labeling email messages, OUT 13, OUT 34
launching apps, OFF 4–5
Links command, PowerPoint Web App, CL 13
Live Preview, OFF 6, OFF 7

M

Mail module, Outlook, OUT 2, OUT 3, OUT 28–29.
    See also email
meetings, OUT 32
message(s)
    email. *See* email
message body, OUT 6, OUT 7
message header, OUT 6, OUT 7
MESSAGE tab
    Address book button, OUT 12
    Attach File button, OUT 14
message threading, OUT 28
Message window, OUT 10, OUT 11
Microsoft Access. *See* Access
Microsoft account, OFF 9
    new, creating, CL 5
    signing in to, CL 4
    signing out of, CL 4
Microsoft Excel. *See* Excel
Microsoft Office. *See also* Access; Excel; PowerPoint; Word
    benefits, OFF 2
    launching apps, OFF 4–5
    moving between programs, OFF 4
    user interface, OFF 6
Microsoft Office 365, OFF 3
Microsoft Office 365 Home Premium edition, OFF 3
Microsoft Outlook. *See* Outlook
Microsoft PowerPoint. *See* PowerPoint
Microsoft SkyDrive. *See* SkyDrive
Microsoft Windows. *See* Windows *entries*
Microsoft Word. *See* Word

N

Navigation Options dialog box, OUT 26, OUT 27
Navigation pane, OUT 26
New Appointment window, OUT 33
New Email button, OUT 6, OUT 14
New Folder button, OUT 9
New Note button, OUT 36, OUT 37
Next Appointment button, OUT 32
note(s)
    copying, OUT 36
    dragging, OUT 36
    thumbnail versions, OUT 36
Notes module, OUT 36–37

O

Office Clipboard, OFF 5
Office Web Apps, CL 2, CL 12–13
OneNote, Office Web App, CL 12

online collaboration, OFF 2, OFF 9
Open as Copy option, Open dialog box, OFF 10
Open dialog box, OFF 10, OFF 11
opening
    files, OFF 10, OFF 11
Open-Read-Only option, Open dialog box, OFF 10
OPTIONS tab, viewing message options, OUT 15
Outbox folder, OUT 8, OUT 9
Outlook
    Calendar module, OUT 27, OUT 32–33
    categories, OUT 40–41
    contact management, OUT 30–31
    coordinating calendars, OUT 41
    email. *See* email
    Mail module, OUT 2, OUT 3, OUT 28–29. *See also* email
    Notes module, OUT 36–37
    overview, OUT 26–27
    People Pane, OUT 26, OUT 27, OUT 38–39
    personal accounts, OUT 26
    Reading Pane, OUT 26, OUT 27
    sending contact information, OUT 33
    setting up, OUT 6
    Tasks module, OUT 34–35
    text editor, OUT 6, OUT 7
Outlook Today, customizing, OUT 37

P

Paragraph command, PowerPoint Web App, CL 13
pasting, Office Clipboard, OFF 5
Peek feature, OUT 32
People module, OUT 30–31
People Pane, OUT 26, OUT 27, OUT 38–39
personal accounts, OUT 26
PowerPoint, OFF 2, OFF 3.
    filename and file extension, OFF 8
    Office Web App, CL 12–13
PowerPoint Last Viewed Slide setting, CL 2
presentation graphics software. *See* PowerPoint
Presentation Views command, PowerPoint Web App, CL 13
previewing
    documents, OFF 12
    email messages, OUT 10
Previous Appointment button, OUT 32
Print command
    PowerPoint Web App, CL 13
Print Layout view, OFF 12
privacy, social networking, OUT 38–39
Properties dialog box, OUT 15

Q

Quick Access toolbar, OFF 6, OFF 7
    customizing, OFF 12
Quick Steps group, Message window, OUT 10, OUT 11

R

Reading Pane
    buttons, OUT 12
    Forward button, OUT 12
    Navigation Pane, OUT 26, OUT 27

Reply All option, Message window, OUT 10
Reply option, Message window, OUT 10
Ribbon, OFF 6, OFF 7
roaming settings, CL 2
rule(s), email, OUT 28, OUT 29
Rules and Alerts dialog box, OUT 28
Rules Wizard, OUT 28, OUT 29

S

Save As command
    PowerPoint Web App, CL 13
Save As dialog box, OFF 8, OFF 9, OFF 10, OFF 11
saving files, OFF 8, OFF 9, OFF 10, OFF 11
    SkyDrive. See saving files to SkyDrive
saving files to SkyDrive, OFF 9
    default, disabling, CL 6, CL 7
screen captures, OFF 13
Select Names: Contacts dialog box, OUT 12
Send/Receive All Folders button, OUT 8, OUT 10, OUT 12
SEND/RECEIVE tab, Send/Receive All Folders button, OUT 8,
    OUT 10, OUT 12
Sent Items folder, OUT 8, OUT 9
Share command, PowerPoint Web App, CL 13
sharing files
    SkyDrive, CL 10–11
shortcut(s), email, OUT 16
shortcut keys, OFF 4
SkyDrive, CL 2, CL 6–7
    accessing, CL 8
    file management, CL 8–9
    saving files. See saving files to SkyDrive
    sharing files, CL 10–11
Slides command, PowerPoint Web App, CL 13
Snipping Tool, OFF 13
social connectors, OUT 38–39
social networking, OUT 38–39
    privacy, OUT 38–39
software
    email, OUT 2
sorting
    email, OUT 28–29
spam, OUT 8
Start screen, OFF 4, OFF 5
starting
    apps, OFF 4, OFF 5
store-and-forward technology, OUT 2
subject line, OUT 6, OUT 7
Subject text box, OUT 6
subscriptions, Microsoft Office 365, OFF 3
suites, OFF 2
syncing, CL 2
system clipboard, OFF 13

T

tab(s)
    Ribbon, OFF 6, OFF 7
task(s), OUT 34
Tasks module, OUT 34–35

templates, OFF 4
Text command, PowerPoint Web App, CL 13
text editors, OUT 6, OUT 7
theme(s), OFF 2
Themes command, PowerPoint Web App, CL 13
thumbnail versions, notes, OUT 36
title bar, OFF 6, OFF 7
To text box, OUT 6
To-Do Bar, OUT 26, OUT 27
To-Do List, OUT 34, OUT 35
top-level domains, OUT 4, OUT 5
touch mode, enabling, OFF 15
Touch Mode button, OFF 15
TRANSITIONS tab
    PowerPoint Web App, CL 13
Transitions to This Slide command, PowerPoint Web App, CL 13

U

UI (user interface), OFF 2
user interface (UI), OFF 2
usernames, OUT 4, OUT 5

V

vacation responses, email, OUT 11
view(s), OFF 12–13. See also specific view names
    changing, OUT 30
View buttons, OFF 12
VIEW tab, OFF 12
    PowerPoint Web App, CL 13
viewing, OFF 12, OFF 13

W

weather information, Outlook Calendar module, OUT 27
Windows Live ID, CL 5. See also Microsoft account
Windows 7, starting apps, OFF 4, OFF 5
Word, OFF 2, OFF 3. See also document(s)
    filename and file extension, OFF 8
    Office Web App, CL 12
Word resume Reading Position setting, CL 2
working online, CL 4–5

Y

Your Profile page, CL 4

Z

Zoom button, OFF 6
Zoom slider, OUT 30
zooming in, OFF 6
zooming out, OFF 6